CLARE
OF ASSISI

GENTLE WARRIOR

WENDY MURRAY

San Damiano Books

PARACLETE PRESS
BREWSTER, MASSACHUSETTS

2020 First Printing

Clare of Assisi: Gentle Warrior

Copyright © 2020 by Wendy Murray
Cat drawing by Jon Zoba

ISBN 978-1-64060-183-3

Cover image: "Santa Chiara" (Opera Unica) by Elvio Marchionni.
70 x 77.5 cm. Mixed media on plaster. Used by permission.

The Paraclete Press name and logo (dove on cross) and the San Damiano Books logo
are trademarks of Paraclete Press, Inc.

Library of Congress Cataloging-in-Publication Data
Names: Murray, Wendy, 1956- author.
Title: Clare of Assisi : gentle warrior / Wendy Murray, author of A mended
and broken heart: the life and love of Francis of Assisi.
Description: Brewster , Massachusetts : San Damiano Books, Paraclete Press,
2020. | Includes bibliographical references and index. | Summary: "Clare
is shown as a figure of true heroism, tenacity, beatitude and grit who
plotted her improbable course in the context of the raucous and
explosive period of the Middle Ages"-- Provided by publisher.
Identifiers: LCCN 2020006805 | ISBN 9781640601833 (trade paperback)
Subjects: LCSH: Clare, of Assisi, Saint, 1194-1253. | Poor Clares--History.
| Poor Clares--Biography. | Franciscans--Biography. | Christian women
saints--Italy--Assisi--Biography. | Christian
saints--Italy--Assisi--Biography.
Classification: LCC BX4700.C6 M87 2020 | DDC 271/.97302 [B]--dc23
LC record available at https://lccn.loc.gov/2020006805

10 9 8 7 6 5 4 3 2 1

Published by Paraclete Press
Brewster, Massachusetts
www.paracletepress.com

Printed in the United States of America

CONTENTS

ABBREVIATIONS

All material taken from *Francis of Assisi: Early Documents* and *Clare of Assisi: Early Documents* is denoted in the notes as *FA:ED* and *CA:ED*, respectively.

1LAg The First Letter to Blessed Agnes of Prague (1234)
2LAg The Second Letter to Blessed Agnes of Prague (1235)
3LAg The Third Letter to Blessed Agnes of Prague (1238)
4LAg The Fourth Letter to Blessed Agnes of Prague (1253)
FLCl The Form of Life (1253)
TestCl The Testament (1247–1253)
BlCl The Blessing
PrPov The *Privilege of Poverty* of Pope Gregory IX (1228)
FLInn The Form of Life provided by Pope Innocent IV (1247)
PC The Acts of the *Process* of Canonization (1253)
VL The Versified Legend (1254–1255)
BC The Bull of Canonization (1254)
LCl The Legend of Saint Clare (1254–1255)

Franciscan Biographical Writings
1C The First Witness of Thomas of Celano (1228)
2C The Second Witness of Thomas of Celano (1245–1247)
AP The Witness of the "Anonymous of Perugia" (1240–1241)
L3C The Legend of the Three Companions (1241–1247)
AC The Assisi Compilation (1244–1260)
LJS The Life of Saint Francis, Julian of Speyer
MP Mirror of Perfection
LegMaj Major Legend of Bonaventure
VL The Versified Life of Saint Francis by Henri d'Avranches

PREFACE

uring a recent visit to Assisi, I chatted frequently with a British couple with whom I shared a breakfast table at the guest house where we were staying. After three breakfasts, they realized I had already written a book about Saint Francis and that the book happened to be available for purchase in the library of the guest house. On their last morning in Assisi, before this couple began the long trek hauling their bags to the train station, the gentleman asked if I would sign the copy of my book he had purchased from the library, which I was happy to do. And off they went. Then, as if in an afterthought, his wife quickly returned to tell me, with wetness in her eyes: "After speaking with you, I understand the feeling I had when I visited San Damiano." (San Damiano is the small convent below town that Francis rebuilt and where Clare of Assisi lived out her days.) I asked her, "What feeling?" She said, "I felt sadness there, almost as if someone had died."

I probed my memory trying to recall what I had said that had awakened such clarity on her part. I recalled, faintly, that I had shared with them how Saint Francis, near the end of his life, had been essentially kicked out of his own religious order,[1] suggesting that the shifting tides of change were overtaking the idealism of his original vision.

The British woman's words hung over me as I continued my research on Saint Clare. By the end of my trip, I felt a similar sadness. I felt it

---

1 See my book, *A Mended and Broken Heart: The Life and Love of Francis of Assisi* (New York: Basic Books, 2008), 123–33. Hereafter, *Mended*.

when I stood in the Basilica of Saint Clare, with its vaulted ceilings covered top-to-bottom in whitewash, with only a few partial glimpses of old frescoes underneath the white in random spots. The story of Clare must have certainly been told through fresco cycles, as was the case of the Basilica of Saint Francis on the other side of town—this was the function and purpose of basilicas. Yet, if there had been any frescoes depicting Clare's life, they had been covered over. I overheard a tour guide explain it, saying that in the sixteenth and seventeenth centuries, during two separate outbreaks of the plague, the basilica had been turned into a hospital and the whitewash was installed for hygienic and cleaning purposes. He added that there was no intention to restore the artwork underneath. Clare's story, he said, was hidden beneath the whitewash and there it would remain.[2] This made me sad.

Where you are still able to find images of Clare in frescoes out and about in Assisi, most depict her as thick-jawed, sometimes dour, and wrapped heavily in black. Yet Clare was beautiful—she was the town beauty in Assisi during her youth—and many men, Francis among them, were enamored of her. She was light-filled and brave, kind and lively. Even before her commitment to a religious life, she gave food to the poor from her table in the *palazzo* in Assisi's wealthy neighborhood of San Rufino. She dismissed out of hand, even as a young maiden, expectations and overtures of betrothal that befit a woman of rank in that town. But the Clare you see in the frescoes show her to be stern, maybe a little dowdy, and sometimes skulking, like a caricature of the nuns you hear about in stories of Catholic boarding schools. This, too, caused me sadness.

Yet, there is one fresco that is extravagantly displayed around town being marketed as the image of Clare. It is a portrait by the pre-Renaissance artist Simone Martini, who painted several portraits of members of the noble and regal class who followed Saint Francis. One portrait among these five depicts a stately woman whose visage is calm

2 A Third Order female Franciscan I spoke with, who gave tours in the Basilica, questioned whether there were frescoes beneath the whitewash.

and lovely; she is draped in delicate linens and crowned with a corona of stars (see page 196). You see it everywhere in Assisi—on postcards, ceramics, in any number of diverse artistic reproductions. This image, of all images, captures the evanescent beauty and dignity of Clare. The problem is, the image is not Clare. Though it is marketed aggressively as Clare, the face belongs to another devoted female follower of Francis who, like Clare, was a woman of rank: Jacopa dei Settisoli, who hailed from Rome and was with Francis when he died. We know this because the corona surrounding the face, mentioned above, is not a crown of stars but of *suns,* and there are seven of them ("Settisoli" means "seven suns" in Italian). When I was researching my book on Saint Francis years ago, I had asked the friar who was the leading expert on the art of the Basilica about the anomaly. Why did they perpetuate, falsely, the image of Jacopa dei Settisoli as being that of Clare when they knew it not to be so? He answered with a shrug. "It is what the people want."[3]

In that moment I understood that, in attempting to research and write honestly about the lives of both Francis and Clare, I would be up against an institutional willingness to embellish, exaggerate, and possibly misrepresent the lives of these personalities in service to "what the people want."

I encountered a similar frustration during my research of Francis. Upon his death, his first official biographer, Thomas of Celano, wrote in 1228 a fairly honest account of Francis's life, including his extravagant and misspent youth. Francis, "maliciously advancing beyond all of his peers in vanities, proved himself a more excessive inciter of evil and a zealous imitator of foolishness. He was an object of admiration to all, and he endeavored to surpass others in his flamboyant display of vain accomplishments: wit, curiosity, practical jokes and foolish talk, songs, and soft and flowing garments. Since he was very rich, he was not greedy but extravagant, not a hoarder of money but a squanderer of his property,

3   See *Mended,* 181.

a prudent dealer but a most unreliable steward."[4] Within a few years this version was eschewed and Thomas of Celano was instructed to write a second biography, which he composed in 1247. This later version, titled *Remembrances* (also called the *Second Life*) glossed over or eliminated altogether references to Francis's rowdy and carnal youth, contrasting starkly to his earlier account. Describing Francis's youth, he now says, "He completely rejected anything that could sound insulting to anyone. No one felt a young man of such noble manners could be born of the stock of those who were called his parents."[5]

Then Bonaventure, who became the Order's Minister General in 1257, ordered all previous versions of Francis's life destroyed in deference to his own *Major Life* (1263), in which he wrote of Francis's youth: "While living among humans, he was an imitator of angelic purity."[6] So it is a long and arduous exercise—tracking the distortions and deciphering the nub of the story beneath the distortions. That is the challenge and heartbreak of the researcher of Francis and Clare. Funny how a simple, devoted British woman, without any knowledge of these things, felt it anyway when she visited the place where Clare lived. Something had died, or, at the very least, gone missing.

I mean no disrespect to those upon whom it has fallen to manage these legacies, even as I attempt to peel away the layers of finessing that have changed and in parts obscured the story of Clare. As one historian put it when we spoke of these matters, "You have to respect the establishment." And that is true. For, without "the establishment," I and you would not have access to libraries and frescoes and friars and lovely vistas as we make our pilgrimages to learn something of Francis and Clare. Yet, ever since that moment when that gifted and helpful scholar-friar freely and unabashedly admitted to me that they perpetuated a falsehood to keep

4   *1C* 1:2; *FA:ED*, vol. 1, 183.
5   *2C*, 1:5, *FA:ED* vol. 2, 242.
6   *LegMaj, FA:ED* vol. 2, 527.

the people happy, I stopped accepting unequivocally the "received text" of the story of Clare.

Thankfully, there is enough that can be known from a few early sources to lend a little ground to stand upon. It is not a lot, but it is enough to begin to understand her on her own terms and not on those foisted upon her by the overseers, both during her life and after her death. These bits, measured against the backdrop of the times in which she lived both politically and ecclesiastically, begin to reveal the shape of her. We see a young, marriageable teenager who ran away from her noble household to follow a young upstart who had embarrassed his own family with a public display of renouncing them. Then, a lifetime later, we see a cloistered, hobbled "nun" (a term she eschewed) who, by that point, had lost every dream, whose life had been reduced to a shadow of her former self, that self who once flew fleet-footed across the plain in the middle of the night to the waiting Francis. Loss upon loss, that young girl died along the way. Time worked its ravages, and Clare had to adapt to sometimes jarringly contradictory circumstances. Yet, with her final breath, she uttered the final benediction of her life: "God, you are blessed for having created me."

How she got from being the fleet-footed teen to the bed-ridden nun—culminating in the benediction that God himself was blessed in creating her—is the exploration of this book. I write it to honor her, the one in whom Francis's soul found rest. The shifting sands of time and intention have changed and obscured her story. I cannot claim to have fully found it or reclaimed her. But I join the orchestra of searchers and scholars and lovers of Francis who have tried against other forces to shake loose the shards of light that remain untouched and which, viewed at the right angle, still shine.

WHY CARE ABOUT CLARE?

have pondered why anyone should care to read a book about the life of Saint Clare. Was she not a derivative of Saint Francis, the truly important figure in this story? What more can she bring to the story that has not already been told in his? Further, she lived in the Middle Ages, an alien time to us; and she, as a woman of rank, willingly, purposefully exchanged a powerful identity for an inglorious one. In these modern times, why would such insouciance arouse curiosity? For others who (like myself) are Protestant, what about the fact that Clare is a "Catholic saint"? Doesn't this mean her story belongs in the cavernous chambers of sacred imagination of Holy Rome, the accoutrements of which the Reformers threw out the Wittenberg door in 1517? By these standards, there is no compelling reason why a modern person, religious or otherwise, would have an interest in this oddly hewn character cut from the rock of medieval Umbria.

Yet, of course there are compelling reasons to study the life of Clare. First, while it could be said that she was derivative of Francis—she was called his "little plant"—Francis died young and Clare was left holding his legacy in her delicate hands while the winds of change and tumult battered the bulwark of his legacy. She fought those battles without him. Beyond that, as one Franciscan historian put it, "In some way we obtain from Saint Clare a clear and more undistracted view of the inner life of the pure Franciscan spirit, than from even Saint Francis himself, since even in him the external duties of the friar are apt somewhat to dim the vision of that interior life which was the innermost sanctuary and nursing ground of the Franciscan spirit."[7] Second, regarding the obscurity of the Middle Ages,[8] I contend that the era is not as alien to our time as one might at first presume. "Barbarities laid bare" might describe either epoch in equitable measure. How does a person of religious conviction live out those ideals in a barbaric age? Clare helps answer that. Third, as for Clare being a woman who renounced power rather than striving to advance it, she offers an alternative picture of femininity that, in an upside-down way, rendered a different kind of power sufficient to shut the mouths of popes and turn advancing armies on their heels. This radical and totally original picture of womanhood will expand the soul of any twenty-first-century feminist. Finally, though Clare was Catholic, it is worth remembering that the Roman Church, in her day, was the only organizing apparatus for Christians, and unless one found protection and identity in that system, one was deemed a heretic. It is a tragedy of the Protestant movement that "the saints" are (at best) ignored and (at worst) dismissed from the faith tradition. One writer said it this way: "It is a cruel injustice and ingratitude to pass by in silence . . . generations of indomitable laborers who had cleared the thorns from the souls of our fathers, as they cleared the soil of Christian Europe."[9] Over the millennia, the "saints"—Clare among them—have risen to the top of global Christian witness, cultivating the landscape of Christian devotion, spawning movements that have changed their worlds.

Yet, I return to my original thought: In the end, there is no compelling *rationale* for any interest in Clare. Curiosity must ultimately arise from a place of mystery and the suspension of the standard categories and rationality. For this is the place where we will truly meet Clare—in the

---

7   Cuthbert, Father, osfc, *Romanticism of St. Francis* (New York: Longmans, Green & Co.,1915), 81.

8   The Middle Ages cover the period of approximately a thousand years between the fall of Rome in the fifth century and the dawn of the Renaissance in (approximately) the fifteenth century.

9   Charles de Montalembert, *The Monks of the West from St. Benedict to St. Bernard*, Vol. 1 (New York: P.J. Kennedy, 1912), 3.

landscape of mystery—that is, if we are courageous enough to go there or desperate enough to end up there.

You Cannot Dream of Clare Without Francis

Years ago, a Franciscan friar in Assisi said to me, "You cannot dream of Clare without Francis, and you cannot dream of Francis without Clare." If you have picked up this book as an introduction to the person of Clare of Assisi, to stay true to the sentiment of that friar, and since it is impossible to understand Clare without a cursory understanding of who he was, I include a brief synopsis of the life of Saint Francis.

Francis of Assisi was born in 1182 and died in 1226. He was a man of his place: Assisi, in the heart of Umbria, Italy, a land of rolling landscapes and a town cascading down the eastern slope of a mystical mountain, Mount Subasio. Assisi was a place that luminesced with magical light and the power of the land at every turn, and this magic animated Francis's heart and imagination.

He lived in the lower part of town, called *il sotto*, the side of town where the merchants and other working people lived. (The nobility, including Clare's family, lived in *la sopra*, the upper side of town.) Francis took great civic pride in his identity as part of the rising merchant class there. He was the son of a wealthy linen merchant and was being groomed to take over the family business, all while showcasing the latest flamboyant styles from France. He was exceedingly popular among Assisi's younger crowd, who crowned him "king of the party." He was a partier and womanizer and often kept the neighbors up at night and turned many heads.

He was also a warrior who aspired to knighthood. The only way a member of the merchant class could achieve that rank was in combat. To that end, he was an active participant in two wars that occurred during his lifetime. The first was a civil war between Assisi's nobility and the merchant class when Francis was 16. During this siege Francis and his fellow merchant-class warriors tore down the walls of the city's main fortress and drove the nobles from their homes into exile, including

Clare's family, raising the banner for the rising merchant class and decisively repulsing entrenched feudalism. The other war, when he was 20, was a melee with the town's rival city, Perugia, and the exiled *Assisiani* nobles, who wanted to reclaim their homes. His friends and fellow warriors were slaughtered during this battle, but Francis survived. Because he was mounted and wearing armor, the enemy deemed him a good candidate for ransom and so took him a prisoner of war. He languished for a year in a dungeon prison with little light, no latrine, and rampant contagions being spread throughout. He became sick to the point of near death during this time until his father ransomed him. It took another year of his life to recover at home under the care of his mother. This changed him. His partying ways subsided and he turned his thoughts to God.

During this season, he became a man of stone, not for the destruction of a fortress, but for rebuilding ruined churches. His sufferings had awakened religious pining. As a result of a vision he had while praying in the ruins of a church outside Assisi, in which he heard the voice of God say to him, "Rebuild my church," he went to work on three ruined churches in the valley below Assisi. The first, San Damiano (where he heard those words, "Rebuild my church"), he intended from the start to be a place to house women. The second is lost[10] and the third, the Porziuncola, became his dwelling place and would eventually become the seat of his young Order.

Francis was very close to the land. He felt its power and perceived God's beauty through every aspect of creation. He often retreated to secluded woods and caves when he needed spiritual centering and peace. He walked lonely mountain roads and had his most intense religious experiences when alone in nature and among the elements.

10 The second church Francis rebuilt was located in the valley below Assisi not far from San Damiano. It was called at the time San Pietro della Spina. In the summer of 2007, an American Franciscan friar and I spent a day trying to locate the ruins of this lost church, which were said to still exist. After several hours of driving around and asking lots of questions to local farmers, we located it, though it was in ruins and overgrown with weeds and undergrowth.

At the end of his life, suffering from many illnesses, he wrote the first lyrical poem in vernacular Italian and put it to music, his famous Canticle of the Creatures (discussed in more detail in chapter 5). He died at the age of 44, within a year of the song's creation. This is the basic outline of his life.

Even if, as it is said, "you cannot dream of Francis without Clare," the person of Clare can still feel elusive. She felt elusive to me, even while I was writing my book about Saint Francis. I could not grasp the woman she became after the death of her beloved friend. She was writing excessively about eternal virginity and spiritual matrimony and beatific poverty, all of it on a level of imagination that felt to me like over-reach. Her spiritual vision of bejeweled breasts and perpetual virginity did not move or touch me. As a result, there always came a point in my research beyond which Clare seemed inaccessible and I abandoned hope of really understanding her. This was necessary at the time, for my mandate then was to focus on the life of Francis. Beyond how Clare's life intersected his, I did not pursue further study of her. Yet now, ten years later—at a different stage of my life and vocation—my thoughts have returned to her.

Francis died when Clare was in her thirties. Prior to then, after she followed him in worldly renunciations as a teen, he tucked her safely away in the monastery of San Damiano—the first of three churches he had rebuilt—and there she would remain, protected by him and provided for by his friars. She sewed altar cloths and prayed for the sick; she performed works of mercy and tended her garden. Yet, despite the seeming tranquility of her new station, she experienced many trials as her life as a penitent religious evolved. (This will be discussed at length in due course.) During the early years of her new life, one of her greatest trials, according to one friar I consulted, was Clare's always being "mad at" Francis because he rarely visited her at San Damiano. Before illness claimed his mobility, Francis was forever on the move throughout Italy and beyond, to Egypt and probably the

Holy Land. This would be the first of many life-shattering adjustments she would navigate as the founding member of Francis's female Order. Francis did return to San Damiano near the end of his life when he was very ill and near death. It was during this brief interlude of his life, in the company of Clare and in her garden, that Francis wrote his great Canticle of the Creatures. This was the last occasion they would see one another. Francis died the next year, becoming increasingly sick and infirm even as Clare was developing a crippling physical malady. By age 34, her approximate age when Francis died, she had become bedridden and was destined to live out her days within the confines of her convent dormitory unless otherwise moved by helpers in attendance.

Yet even from her bed, Clare bushwhacked her way into uncharted territory, both for women's religious societies generally and Francis's version of penitence specifically. She created new terms and differing themes for an existence that transcended the terms and themes of the Middle Ages and the rules of the Church. She broke through the social and religious apparatus that defined her times and she broke through her physical challenges. Clare is a breaker-through-er. She scaled high mountains from the confines of a little room in a modest convent that rested on a sloping hill outside the small town that had been her home. She could no longer walk, and she had renounced the securities of her noble rank. Yet she turned her world upside-down.

Clare is one for whom all earthly dreams evaporated and all imaginings for who she might become were consigned to some other place. That "other place" is where the real story of Clare begins. Real life kept Clare pinned to earth, but true life found her in that hidden place, the same place we all end up when there is no place left to go.

She has left an echo that reverberates to this day. It is a true echo, a clear echo. That is what makes her story meaningful now. If Clare could break through the terms dictated by her times and circumstances, surely we ought to be able to break through ours.

Every spiritual seeker is a prisoner of time. Similarly, the attempt to believe enough to try and know God and to live for him must begin in time, in one's own time, on a date on the calendar of one's own history. We are all of us prisoners of the time in which we live. That is a place of commonality where she, in her time, and we in ours, can meet in friendship. And more than friendship, it is where we can reclaim life—our true life—amid a world gone amuck.

||||||||||||||||||||||||||||||||||||||||||||

Part
One

||||||||||||||||||||||||||||||||||||||||||||

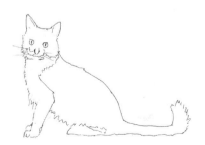

||||||||||||||||||||||||||||||||||||||||||||||

NOBILITY

It is impossible to grasp the significance of Clare and the power of her story without first understanding the rock from which she was hewn. And here, alas, the researcher runs into heartbreak.

What little historical knowledge we have of Saint Clare is derived largely from the early Franciscan documents, most of which interpreted her life through the life of Saint Francis. Even in these early writings, however, mention of Clare began to disappear over time. Franciscan scholar Paschal Robinson noted despairingly: "Not a few [records] were destroyed; others disappeared. As far as dates go, only one—the date of her canonization—is given. Save for a few fragments of pious legend not one of the early sources gives us the year of Saint Clare's birth. . . . [W]e are without any exact knowledge of the life of Saint Clare down to 1212."[11]

Within two years after Francis's death at the age of 44 in 1226 (when Clare was approximately 34) the process of his canonization hastily took place and multiple narratives about the saint emerged, written by a diverse company of biographers for varying audiences.[12] This period also marks the time when the role of Clare in his story began to be diminished and in some instances excised altogether. As Francis's story evolved, the

---

11 Paschal Robinson, OSF, *"Saint Clare,"* from *Franciscan Essays* by Paul Sabatier and others (Aberdeen, UK: Aberdeen University Press, 1912), 35.

12 Details denoting the hasty canonization *process* are delineated in Jacques Dalarun, *The Misadventure of Francis of Assisi: Toward a Historical Use of the Franciscan Legends,* trans. Edward Hagman (Saint Bonaventure, NY: Franciscan Institute Publications, 2002), 124ff.

presence of Clare in his story diminished.[13] For a variety of reasons, the creation of the saint meant the separation of her from his story. One historian in Assisi I spoke with told me, "Saint Clare was dangerous for the Church, so they tried to separate the two lives. She was too strong. Clare could be very problematic."[14]

Despite critical gaps in the historical record about her, there remain elements of her life we do know incontrovertibly. We know, for example, that she was born into Assisi's nobility and so enjoyed great advantages in her early life. We know she lived in a family of knights who were courageous, industrious, magnanimous, and cruel. We know she was born and grew up in Assisi (with an interlude, in exile, in neighboring Perugia), an intimate, feisty town hungry for war and where families and neighbors stood with one another in games and, at times, against one another in warfare. In either case, honor of the local saints wove the fabric of civic life together, whether San Rufino, San Giorgio, or Santo Stefano.[15] She was surrounded by the women of Assisi who were resolute and impassioned and took pilgrim journeys overseas and who, when needed, joined in battle and went on Crusades. We know she was the firstborn daughter of a woman of noble lineage, Ortolana, devout, daring, and indomitable: as a young woman Ortolana traveled the pilgrim route from Assisi to Damietta (Egypt) to Mount Sinai and on to the Holy Land, where Saracen bandits continually harassed the traveling bands.

Clare lived in the Middle Ages when general barbarities of society and politics were laid bare. People knew the terms, knew what side they were on, and stood their ground ready to defend and die on that ground, which often was the case. There is something to be said for barbarities

13 Clare's important role in Francis's life is acknowledged by all of his biographers. However, the scope and depth of the relationship is absent from their official biographies. Clare is honored in her own right in a separate legend attributed to Thomas of Celano. But their lives, as denoted in the official written record, were tracked separately.

14 Simone Fanelli, historian and official guide in Assisi; personal interview, November 2007.

15 For more information on the role of the saints in Assisi's civic identity see *Mended*, 12–14.

that are laid bare as opposed to barbarities that pulsate beneath the surface, under appearances, proclamation, and societal grievance, as is the case in our day. "Let's just have it out" was the way of public discourse in the Middle Ages, which sometimes resulted in a call to arms but just as often left towns and their inhabitants to live and let live. War was intimate and endemic, both locally—town against town—and globally. Combat, carnage, and death were woven into the culture and were almost considered a rite of passage, especially for male members of the nobility who were born into knighthood or for those outside the noble class but who aspired to it. Knighthood was steeped in the culture of chivalry, a notion that loomed large in the imagination of the age. The nearness of death stripped away moral equivocation about it. It was a given that men would die (women too), and probably young. To die in principled combat conferred honor on their lives and glory upon their deaths. Thus, inherent in the culture of war and death was the disposition of courage. "Luxury" among the nobles was not a pillow to be sat upon. The members of the families of highest rank were knights, and sometimes women would engage in combat, too. Even Saint Francis had early aspirations of knighthood, engaged in brutal warfare, and inevitably took human life as a matter of course. In the time of Francis and Clare, "fighting the good fight" was not a theological abstraction. It involved arms, lances, shields, scabbards, and swords. There is a certain lucidity that arises from living a life in which the rules of engagement are so clearly and unapologetically importuned. Clare—in keeping with her name, which means "light"— possessed such lucidity.

Clare's having been born into a family of great knights meant that warfare was woven into the fabric of her home life. "The sounds of war were ever about her house with the din of iron clad armor and longswords struck against floors."[16] Ancestors on her father's side spawned a powerful family of feudal knights in central Italy and part of the Duchy of Spoleto. (Spoleto is a nearby hill town that served like the county seat.) The family names first appear in civic records in 1106, naming the sons of "Offredo" as Bernardo and Monaldo.[17] Bernardo (sometimes referred to as Bernardino) had two sons—Offreduccio and Rinaldo—the first of whom was Clare's paternal grandfather.[18] He, in turn, had five sons, a cavalcade of knights: Monaldo (who appears later in Clare's story), Paolo, Ugolino, Scipione, and Favorone—Clare's father. She was known as Chiara di Favorone, daughter of Favorone, son of the well-known Count Offreducio di Bernardino. One of her relatives went on a crusade to fight the Saracens in Egypt, about whom it was recorded: "[O]ne after another he bowled them over; happy were they who showed him their heels because all others were sliced like turnips."[19]

Lineage on her father's side arose from German descent, part Frank and part Lombard. The Lombards were known to be taciturn, strong, decisive, and deeply rooted in a sense of social caste; the Franks were more open to contact and social interaction. Clare possessed positive qualities from both. She was known for her dignity and austerity as well as for her long blond hair (Lombard), but paid little mind to demarcations of social castes. She was also known to have been refined, meek in temperament, and in possession of a certain sweetness about her nobility (Frankish). One writer said: "She possessed that ancient prudence of her ancestors, which often turned into silence."[20]

---

16 Arnaldo Fortini, *Francis of Assisi*, translated by Helen Moak, (New York: Crossroad, 1992), 329. Taken from *Nova Vita di San Francesco*, 4 vols. (Milan, 1926 and Assisi: Tipografia Porziuncola, 1959).

17 *Acts of Assisi;* see Gemma Fortini and Finbarr Conroy, "The Noble Family of St. Clare of Assisi," *Franciscan Studies* Vol. 42 (1982), 48–67.

18 Civic documents dated between 1145 and 1177 exist that show Offreduccio and his brother, Rinaldo, vowing not to increase the height of the family home near the Cathedral of San Rufino. See Fortini, Arnaldo, "New Information Concerning Clare of Assisi," *GR* 7 (1993): 29.

19 Fortini and Conroy, "The Noble Family of St. Clare of Assisi," 48.

20 Fortini and Conroy, "The Noble Family of St. Clare of Assisi," 52.

Favorone, it was said, was a knight "capable of fighting on horseback pursuing bands of the enemy with a drawn sword."[21] Beyond that, little is known about him. In the document tracing interviews made during the process of Clare's canonization, called *The Acts of the Process of Canonization*,[22] one witness, Pacifica di Guelfuccio—who was a blood relative of Clare's—said that she "had never seen" him,[23] while another witness, Pietro di Damiano, says he did know him when Clare was the age of 17—adding that both parents wanted her to marry. Otherwise, Favorone disappears from the narrative of Clare's story. When Clare broke from the family to follow Francis, it was her paternal uncle, Monaldo, who pursued her in the effort to keep the family together. The same is true when her sister Catherine (later Agnes) followed suit. We know that Clare's mother joined her daughter at San Damiano in 1226, the year Francis died, leading some to conclude that Favorone must have already died in order for her to take this step. Arnaldo Fortini makes the case, however, that Favorone may still have been living in the year 1229, since his name appears in archival records that highlight town fugitives. Naming three serfs "belonging to" Favorone, the record states: "Giles, a servant of Favorone, is condemned for his contumacy, because he . . . did not pay his fine of 25 *soldi*. Amicolus, a servant of Favorone, is condemned for the same reason. Bernardicius, a servant of Favorone, is condemned because he did not pay his fine."[24]

One can't help but wonder what kind of father he might have been to his three lovely, marriageable daughters and the kind of husband he was to his irrepressible, adventurous wife. Regardless, when it came to attempting to hold the family together after the intrusion and breakage

---

21 Fortini and Conroy, "The Noble Family of St. Clare of Assisi," 48.

22 This document, called in its entirety *The Acts of the Process of Canonization*, was discovered in 1920 by Zefferino Lazzeri and was published the same year. The text that follows offers an extraordinary glimpse into details of Clare's life, before and after her religious vows. I refer to it often, and in the body of the text I will refer to the document simply as *Process* and in the notes as *PC*.

23 *PC*, 1,4; *CA:ED*, 145.

24 Fortini, "New Information," 36.

caused by the one-time town playboy, Francesco, it was Monaldo who undertook it. But he failed.

An absentee father notwithstanding, no person informed Clare's understanding of womanhood, chivalry, and Christian devotion more than her mother, Ortolana, a great adventurer and devoted pilgrim. Ortolana was born from the same familial line as the German Emperor Frederick II (who was born in Assisi December 26, 1195, near the same time of Clare's birth[25]) and married her distant cousin, the accomplished knight, Favorone. Clare's mother would have recounted to her three daughters stories of great knights who undertook glorious battles under the banner of the Cross. At the same time, she modeled a steeled devotion that would later define the spiritual constancy of Clare.

Ortolana came of age under the terms of privilege and responsibility that a noble lineage demanded, yet she was a woman of great faith and not in word only. She put action to her devotion and traveled tirelessly to Christian holy sites on more than one pilgrimage, including sites in Bethlehem and Jerusalem before they had been seized by the Saracens. Being married to an active and accomplished knight, she would have had occasion to accompany him on some of his campaigns and especially on a crusade—one writer notes, "the Crusading armies were habitually encumbered with crowds of non-combatants." She rallied around the then-universal sentiment that the barbarity of the Saracen-usurped sacred Christian sites could not stand so long as there were believers willing to fight for their liberation.

Ortolana embraced the spiritual power of the pilgrimage, which took the believer outside the boundaries of a small world into the grand landscape of the heroes of early Christianity. More than that, the

25 Fortini maintains that Frederick II was born in Assisi, not Iesi, as many scholars wrongly assert: A thirteenth-century Franciscan, Albert of Stade, wrote that Frederick was "born in *valle Spoletana in civitate Asis*. The fact that he mentioned the Spoleto Valley means that he was not guilty of an error in spelling when he wrote Asis instead of Iesi, a city in the Marches of Ancona that is generally held to be his birthplace." Albert further noted that Frederick was baptized in Assisi at the age of three "in the presence of fifteen bishops and cardinals." Fortini/Moak, 108–09.

pilgrimage made tangible the human existence of their beloved Savior, which made pilgrimage in the Middle Ages the primary expression of Christian devotion, routinely forging the souls of great saints, privileged nobles, and average peasants alike. "The uprooting and the physical hardships entailed in going on pilgrimage gave the Christian a chance to atone for his sins and to travel in search of the heavenly homeland," as one writer described it.[26] When the holy sites were usurped and defiled by non-believing Saracens, Ortolana, along with all of Christian Europe, responded with utter dismay and resolve to reclaim these holy places for the name of Christ.

So going on a Crusade was, in essence, a kind of spiritual pilgrimage, both for the knights who raised the banner of the cross and the pilgrims who followed them. "In reality, the Crusades were pilgrimages under arms. . . . The same conviction which impelled the pilgrim to leave home and set out along the roads in search of the heavenly Jerusalem also spurred on the crusaders to free the earthly Jerusalem."[27] To this end, going was considered "the most wonderful adventure in the world . . . *Dieu le veut* (God wills it)."[28] Though the ideals of chivalry animated the effort, "chivalry" would not describe how this effort sometimes played out. But the glories of battle and the aspirations of the knight lay behind the sentiment of the day, the same certitude Ortolana embraced (being married to a knight) as she went on pilgrimage and as her husband went to battle on various Crusades. Ortolana would have imparted to her children stories of her adventures on pilgrimage as well as their transformative power.

It is documented in the testimonies for the *Process* that Ortolana and her friend Pacifica, daughter of Guelfuccio di Bernardo (another noble house of Assisi), made this journey to the Holy Land. The year is presumed to have been 1192, since for a brief period of time peace

26 J. Micó, "The Spirituality of Saint Francis," *GR* 7 (1993), 19.
27 Micó, "The Spirituality of Saint Francis, 19.
28 Nesta De Robeck, *Saint Clare of Assisi* (Chicago: Franciscan Herald Press, 1980), 23.

had been made by the Muslim leader, Saladin, who opened the way for Christians to come to the land he now occupied. This was the only year Saladin allowed Christians to enter Jerusalem.

The standard route on a pilgrimage to the Holy Land took them through Egypt, landing first in the sea town of Damietta—the same port where Francis would travel thirty years later. From there they would proceed through Sinai, where they would climb the holy mountain where Moses received the law and the beloved fourth-century martyr Catherine of Alexandria is interred.

The trip from Damietta to Sinai was a treacherous fifteen-day slog across a harsh desert with Arab guides who seldom could be trusted. In this region, Ortolana and her companions would have traveled without official safe passage granted by the sultan (who gave permission only in Jerusalem) and would have been under constant threat of armed Saracen bandits who lay in wait to assault and attack pilgrims without warning. During such skirmishes, the men would engage in battle while the women would pray for the protection of Saint Catherine. (Praying for the protection of the saints was woven into the spirituality of medieval Christianity.)

Ortolana would have later told her impressionable daughters the tales of her pilgrim's passage and particularly, the story of Saint Catherine. Catherine of Alexandria lived in Alexandria, Egypt, during the fourth century, a period of great persecution under the Roman Emperor Marcus Aurelius Valerius Maxentius. She was a young and devout virgin of noble lineage who strongly protested the persecution of Christians, for which she was imprisoned. Her courage and resolve both during and after her imprisonment inspired many to convert to Christianity, including the emperor's wife. Because of her vast influence, she was brought before Maxentius and (it is said) attested, "I am Catherine, the daughter of the king, and I have abandoned all my riches in order to follow the Lord Jesus Christ." As a result, she was ordered to be tortured and executed, as was the fate of many Christians during that era. The implement of choice was the excruciating torture of the spiked wheel, on which the victim would be tied and then swung across a bed of fire or metal spikes. Because the wheel had spikes mounted on it, pain came from all directions. When Catherine was placed upon the wheel, the story goes, the implement broke, forcing her executioners to improvise. (She was instead beheaded.) Hence, this form of torture has been called "the Catherine wheel," and she has come to be known as Saint Catherine of the Wheel. Since she was martyred in Alexandria, she became the guardian saint over the portion of the pilgrimage journey that traversed Mount Sinai. Ortolana would have prayed for the protection of Saint Catherine on her arduous journey. And traversing the road to Mount Sinai would surely have demanded the supernatural aid of the saints. A fourteenth-century chronicler who made the same pilgrimage said of it: "There is not in all the world a pilgrimage harder than the one to Mount Sinai."[29] Ortolana would also have told her daughters how Saint Catherine of the Wheel guarded the pilgrims.[30]

Shortly after her return to Assisi, Ortolana was either pregnant or soon became pregnant with her first child, for whom she spent many hours before a crucifix in prayer. Under the cross she heard a word from the

---

29 Friar Antonio dei Riboldi described the journey in his work *Itinerarium ad montem Sinai;* see Fortini, 331–32. Arnoldo Fortini describes vividly the "typical" pilgrimage to Mount Sinai: "The pilgrims climbed the lofty peak, bloodying their hands and their feet . . . They looked at the stone that still preserves the imprint of the martyr [Catherine]. Afterwards they went down to the monastery of the Greek monks, who came in procession, joyful and serene. 'There is among them,' says an ancient chronicle, 'admirable peace and harmony, and at the same time, abstinence and prayers, and frequent ringing out of devout psalmodies, which follow a time of sacred silence. It seemed they must lead the life of angels rather than men.'" The pilgrims would be escorted to the church of that monastery, fortified with high towers and commanding walls to defend against the unrelenting assaults by bands of infidels. In that church lay a sarcophagus where reposed the mortal remains of Catherine (according to legend), before which the pilgrims would kneel and kiss. The same chronicler mentioned above wrote, "[Saint Catherine] saved us from dying of thirst and delivered us from the hands of those Arabs—she, for whose devotion our pilgrimage was inspired. Many vows were then made, many prayers recited, many tears shed." Fortini and Moak, 332.

30 It is worth noting that Ortolana named her second daughter Catherine, presumably after the martyred saint who carried them safely as they traversed the holy mountain. It is also notable that there still exists in Assisi, near the home of Clare's family, an ancient monastery dedicated to Saint Catherine, where the townspeople venerated her.

Lord: "Lady, do not fear, because you will bring forth a clear light that will illuminate the world."[31] This would be Clare, her firstborn, named Chiara (Italian for "light") befitting the promise made to Ortolana in prayer.

Clare had two sisters, Catherine (later named Agnes) and Beatrice. The latter wrote that as a young woman, Clare "sold all her inheritance and part of [Beatrice's] and gave it to the poor. Then Saint Francis cut off her hair in front of the altar in the church of the Virgin Mary called the Porziuncola and conducted her to the Church of San Paolo de Abbatissis." Clare, as a young maiden still in the family home, was solicitous toward the poor to the point of selling for their benefit her inheritance and part of her sister's, too.

Assisi's Civil Wars

In 1198, when Clare would have been approximately six years old and Francis 16, Assisi's merchant class incited open rebellion against the nobility, raising their swords in the name of the *comune*,[32] the heretofore unknown concept of democratic rule. Assisi's merchants wanted independence from both the political strong-arming of the Church as well as the dominance of feudal lords, and the town was ready to wage war to claim it. At a strategically opportune moment, when the Empire's delegate had left town, Assisi's merchant-class warriors, Francis among them, laid siege to the seat of political power, Assisi's fortress called La Rocca. This fortress stood high over the upper side of town where the nobles lived—including Clare's family—for the purpose of protecting and defending them. The upstart warriors pulled stone after stone from the fort's white rugged walls until the bulwark was dismantled, leaving the nobility undefended.

---

31 Fortini and Moak, 332.

32 The rise of the *comune* (commune) was the portent of the demise of feudalism. The merchant class, or *mediani*, fueled the movement with aspirations of winning their share of the prize heretofore claimed exclusively by the nobility, the *maggiori*—that is, upward mobility. Their only means of asserting this claim was to make war.

Thus began a civil war in Assisi that soon extended well beyond the destruction of the fortress, spilling onto the city streets. The merchant-warriors routed nearby castles and other strongholds of feudalism in town and the surrounding hills, driving noble families from their homes. Many fled due west to Perugia, Assisi's hated rival city. Clare and her family were among those driven from their homes and castles. It is therefore possible that Francis's first encounter with Clare was in the context of war, terrorizing her and her family and routing them from town.

For the next two years, from 1198 to 1200, Assisi and Perugia existed in a state of guerrilla warfare that included raids, ambushes, border skirmishes, and reprisals.

In November 1202 the displaced noble lords who had been exiled to Perugia decided to take back their city and declared war against Assisi. Always ready for a fight, Assisi answered the challenge. On a brisk November morning, knights and merchant warriors left the city gate led by a chariot bearing the colors of the *comune*, blue and red, with the crest of a lion and a cross. Francis was numbered among the *Campagnia dei Cavalieri*—the city's elite corps of armed companies made up of knights and prosperous merchants who could afford a horse and armor.

The result was a devastating slaughter for Assisi. Most of Francis's partying companions-turned-warriors fell, though Francis survived—a testament to his skill as a rider and warrior. Since he was wearing armor, which suggested wealth, the *Perugini* took him as a prisoner with the expectation of a paid ransom for his release. Francis languished for a year in squalor and fetid conditions with deteriorating health. His father secured his release through payment and Francis came home very near the point of death.

For Clare and her family, the victory of the *Perugini* in the same battle meant, at long last, returning from exile and coming home. The family of Favarone di Offreducci reclaimed their home in Assisi and worked with town officials to establish a new form of governance for the small town, which made official, by law, the birth of the *comune*.[33] More importantly, Favorone began preliminary negotiations to secure a marriage of rank for his eldest and most marriageable daughter. And Clare had many suitors and had received offers of marriage. She is well-known for having refused these, against her parents' will.

Toward Penitence

The historical record goes murky during the years between 1202 and 1204 regarding the lives of Clare and Francis. In *A Mended and Broken Heart*, I make the case that Francis and Clare had come to know one another at this point and in fact grew deeply fond of one another, to the point of breaking social rules in order to meet clandestinely.[34] It is well known, from the testimonies for Clare's canonization, that Francis and Clare often met privately. It is also well-known that Clare, even as a child, had been deeply religious. It is my conviction that Clare was the catalyst arousing Francis's religious pining and that their mutual love fueled Francis's interest in and ultimate conversion to religion. In turn

---

33 Both the merchants and the feudal lords understood that if Assisi was to survive and thrive as a rising commune, there must be reconciliation, so they named arbiters to draw up a document—a Peace Paper: "Because there is in Assisi discord between the [nobility] and the men of the people over the destruction of the castles and feudal servitude." The peace agreement listed the names of feudal lords whose homes had been destroyed, ordered that the commune construct new houses and towers, and outlined the dimensions of the buildings to be erected and the districts that were to be rebuilt. (*Archivio della cattedrale di San Rufino*).

34 This is attested to in the *Process*. In *Mended*, I describe this period as obscure regarding Francis's leanings toward religion. He had been raised in and himself had fully embraced the extravagant lifestyle of the burgeoning merchant class, he had lived his youth driven by the flesh and, coming into manhood, he longed only for the glory of knighthood. Was his change of heart mystical? Or was there a valid secondary agent who encouraged his thinking to go in a new direction? Thomas [of Celano], Francis's first biographer, says Francis spent a lot of time at this point in his life going with an unnamed friend "to remote places, places well-suited for counsel, telling him that he had found a certain precious and great treasure." His friend rejoiced and "willingly accompanied Francis whenever he was asked." Thomas calls this secret friend someone "he loved more than any other because he was the same age." (He identifies him as a man.) He says that because of their "great familiarity" and "mutual affection" Francis shared the secrets of his inner turmoil with him. I have speculated and posed the question if this friend might not have been Clare in the earliest stage of their blossoming friendship. See *Mended*, 36–37.

they struggled with an intractable dilemma: their mutual love and their disparity in rank. This love drove their joint decision to renounce rank and family, become religious penitents, and live out their days in chaste and holy mutuality.

For the next several years,[35] Francis underwent a tortured and yet complete spiritual transformation, renouncing family, wealth, and his former habit of prancing about in flamboyant French linens. He took to building ruined churches while Clare lent financial support.[36] The first building he completed was the small church of San Damiano, just below town. He proclaimed from the outset, before any notion of starting a religious order, that this church would house holy women.[37] Clare indeed eventually took up residency there. Until that time, she and Francis continued to meet secretly; he continued to repair other churches; they continued to make plans.

---

35 Approximately during the years 1205 and 1206.
36 *PC* 17, 7; *CA:ED*, 193.
37 *Mended*, 73.

CHAPTER 2

||||||||||||||||||||||||||||||||||||||||

PINING

It was known around Assisi at that time that Francesco Bernardone—one-time town playboy who had lately taken an eccentric turn—was whispering in Clare's ear. He and Clare had become mutually enamored of one another, in one way or another, and Francis took to visiting her frequently. More to the point, she was visiting him "more frequently": "[She] desired to see and hear him. No less did he desire to see and speak with her. . . . He visited her and she more frequently him."[38]

Beyond this little bit of information, Clare's movements during the few years that preceded her break from the family to join Francis remain obscure. This is especially true of the particular nature of her relationship with Francis. The generally accepted opinion maintains that Clare heard Francis preaching in the piazza near the town Cathedral of San Rufino (which would have been, essentially, outside her front door) and she longed to hear more, a longing that Francis gladly accommodated. The fact is, however, it is not known how Francis and Clare actually met or when she first heard him preach.

As already noted, the case can be made that Clare and Francis knew one another long before this version of the story suggests, and that Clare was instrumental in igniting Francis's religious pining and eventual conversion. It took Francis approximately two years of inner turmoil before he "left the world," as he put it, when his conversion culminated in his embracing a leper. This gesture, at long last, slew the beast that throughout his youth had held him captive: his flesh. This decisive event occurred in 1206. This was the same year he had heard a voice speak to him from a dangling crucifix among the ruins of the church of San Damiano commanding him to "rebuild my church." In his typical fashion, Francis took the pronouncement literally and began gathering stones to shore up the walls. This was also the year he became alienated from his father because of his efforts on the church's behalf and the year he took a pilgrimage to Rome. Religious pining was doing its work upon him.

Was Clare a part of this picture at that time? We know that from the earliest days of his rebuilding enterprise at San Damiano, Francis intended the structure to house women, though he had given no indication at that point of any intention to establish a new religious order. Even so, he broadcast his intention to house women long before his new allegiance had attracted followers.[39] We also know that, in the few years following his work on San Damiano (1207 and 1208), he likewise went to work repairing two other ruined churches, San Pietro della Spina and the Porziuncola. It has been recorded that Clare gave Francis funds out of her own purse to help with the latter. By late 1208 he had attracted a few local men of high rank who followed him in his religious vows. In early 1209, he still did not know how this new movement would evolve and it had not yet become an official Order.

So, at the very least, the fact that Francis proclaimed his earliest church restoration project to be for the eventual use of women, coupled with the fact that Clare was supporting him financially, strongly suggests not only that she knew him, possibly during the years of his religious pining, but especially in the immediate aftermath of his conversion, and

---

39 "While laboring with others in that work, he used to cry to passers-by in a loud voice, filled with joy, saying in French: 'Come and help me in the work of the church of San Damiano which, in the future, will be a monastery of ladies through whose fame and life our heavenly Father will be glorified.'" *L3C*, in *FA:ED* vol. II, 83.

that they shared a bond of trust and friendship. This, in turn, suggests their relationship was both long-standing and intimate.[40]

Penitential religious movements

Whatever the thoughts and plans that Francis and Clare contrived about the timing of her dramatic move, they both benefitted from and were perhaps emboldened by a confluence of factors, one of which medieval scholar Paul Sabatier has called "a hurricane" that was sweeping over Europe in the Middle Ages: "Each body of water has its own currents, but when the hurricane is abroad they mysteriously intermingle, and from the ocean to the remotest mountain lake the same tremor will upheave them all." The hurricane sweeping over the religious landscape in the Middle Ages were the tides of religious reform that were sweeping across Europe in the thirteenth century.

One such reform movement—and the one that shaped Francis's spiritual vision—was called the *Ordo Poenitentium* (Order of Penitents). This reform movement is credited for the proliferation of monasteries and hermitages that gained wide popularity in the twelfth and thirteenth centuries among laity, clergy, oblates, hermits, and pilgrims. Its devotion showed itself through poverty, mendicant preaching, and acts of mercy toward outcasts and lepers. Early on, as the movement gained momentum, the Catholic Church (contending with other distractions) left these expressions of religious enthusiasm without direction and oversight, and this inevitably contributed to the flowering of heresies and alien offshoots. This in time compelled Church authorities to become

---

40 The case I made in my earlier book was that Clare was at the center of his deepest religious pinings: "When Francis was praying in the caves [during the year 1205], he wrestled with temptation of the flesh. There was also talk among his friends during this time of a girlfriend, which he confirmed. All the while, he was feeling movements of heart that inclined him toward religion. Clare, too, was experiencing spiritual pining, as noted by those who knew her at home. He was advancing in his spiritual vision while she, under his guidance, was advancing in hers. . . . As the story unfolds, it seems apparent that Francis and Clare broke rank together. Out of an increasing love for God and (this writer asserts) in the throes of an unresolved mutual love for each other . . . he acted first and prepared the way for Clare to follow, which she did a few years later." *Mended*, 53–54.

more skeptical about giving legitimacy to these sundry penitential bands, though Francis would be instrumental in overcoming this reticence. Similar reform movements for women likewise flourished during this time. It is this model that most likely inspired Clare to believe she could thrive and succeed in a new vocation as a religious penitent.

Another factor that had to have influenced the thinking of Francis and Clare, and that no doubt benefitted their planning, was the new paradigm for the religious life that was emerging at the time, as a result of these changing winds, for both male and female religious penitents thanks to Saint Benedict of Norcia (c. 480 to c. 547) and his innovative model for a thriving penitential Order for both males and females. In the fifth century, Benedict had laid the groundwork for religious penitents that would still bear fruit in the thirteenth century. He was born in Norcia, Umbria, into a family of Roman nobility, though he despaired of the decadent way of life he experienced during his years of study in Rome. He left the city life, exchanging it instead for a life of reflection, penitence, and prayer. By 529 Benedict had commanded a following and had unintentionally launched an Order that would shape the religious landscape of the Middle Ages. Benedict's teachings emphasized finding God in the ordinary circumstances of daily life, thus introducing the concept of the dignity of manual labor. The Benedictines harnessed rivers by building dams and dikes and tamed the land to make it arable and farmable. Benedict also instituted a regimen of praying several times a day at specific hours, a practice called the Daily Office, which Francis and Clare faithfully adopted. The Benedictines, being rich in land and castles, owned monasteries and little churches throughout Umbria. By the time of Francis and Clare, the Benedictine Order had become strong, well-established, and entrenched in its social standing. Francis's conversion, in fact, had taken place in a run-down abandoned Benedictine church. When he undertook to restore it, and then two other nearby churches, it was the Benedictine abbot of a monastery on Mt. Subasio, called San Benedetto, who secured the properties for Francis.

That he and Clare each had a viable model for how to lead the life of a penitent, and the available real estate to anchor their hopes, set the stage for the first concrete steps they took toward this end.

Francis's early steps

For a long time in the early days of his religious life (approximately 1206 and 1207), Francis undertook the building projects. He worked first on San Damiano and then moved on to two other properties, the Porziuncola and a small church called San Pietro della Spina. At this point in his life he dressed as a penitent in a tunic and sandals and begged for bread and also for stones with which to build. But he had not yet given any shape to his convictions and simply chose for himself to live as a penitent.

The building activity, however, began to attract attention of the locals in Assisi, who had known Francis as a clothier, an aspiring knight, and a ladies' man—not as a beggar. Some townspeople, predictably, dismissed him as mad. Others were moved by his humility, tenacity, and happiness in the face of poverty and ridicule. He began to be approached by citizens of rank who had become curious about his work. Among the first to inquire was a wealthy man of arms named Bernard of Quintavalle, a respected and learned member of the nobility[41] who held degrees in civil and canon law. He owned a home in Assisi not far from Francis's family home, was approximately the same age as Francis, and probably had fought with him in battle. Bernard watched from a distance as surprising changes overtook the erstwhile party-loving son of Pietro Bernardone, and he couldn't make sense of them. He harbored questions and, more than once, invited Francis to stay in his home.

The legends say that one night when Francis was staying in Bernard's home, his host found him not sleeping but praying. This, in Bernard's mind, consummated the mounting evidence that Francis's change was

---

41 Thomas of Celano, Francis's first biographer, mentions an earlier follower about whom little is known. *1 C.* in *FA:ED* vol. I, 203.

authentic and his convictions worthy to be trusted. He resolved to join Francis in the life of a penitent.

Since Bernard was laden with properties in and around Assisi, his desire to embrace poverty left him with a predicament that demanded legal maneuvering. Together he and Francis consulted a man of law in Assisi, a prominent citizen named Peter of Catanio. Peter lived in the neighborhood of the Cathedral of San Rufino among the other nobility (where Clare also lived) and had, like Bernard, been baffled by Francis's strange new allegiance, and was now even more baffled that the respected Bernard of Quintavalle had embraced it. The three men shared many probing conversations, and, in time, Peter expressed the desire likewise to live the penitent life. Together they explored how to appropriate this choice, given their respective social stations. The three set out together to the Church of San Nicolo—a small church that was next door to Francis's childhood home—where Francis knew the priest. The priest read to them from Matthew's Gospel: "If you seek perfection, go, sell your possessions, and give to the poor. Take nothing on the way. If a man wishes to come after me, he must deny his very self."[42] Francis told Peter and Bernard to "go and fulfill everything you have heard," as he himself had already done.

By 1208 or early 1209 a handful of Assisi's noble citizens had voluntarily assumed beggars' garb in order to follow Francis. Eventually known as Assisi's "penitents," they included, among others, Clare's noble cousin Rufino; a troubadour poet known as Pacifico (who was later crowned poet laureate of the empire by Emperor Frederick II); a handsome and eloquent personality named Masseo, who would later harbor jealousy toward Francis; and a knight and minstrel named Angelo, from the great house of Tancredo, a powerful family in Assisi.[43] Leo, who

---

42 Matthew 19:21. They also read from Luke 9:3, "Take nothing for your journey," and Matthew 16:24, "If any man will come after me, let him deny himself."

43 Tancredo was an influential member of Assisi's citizenry and, being fiercely devoted to the ideals of the *comune*, was a member of the governing consul that led the revolt of 1198.

joined the order by 1211, became Francis's scribe, traveling companion, confessor, and his closest and most trusted friend.[44] When these earliest companions had renounced rank and joined Francis, he had been working on the ruined churches and receiving funds from Clare.[45] Even so, he "was still altogether ignorant of how things would turn out for him and his new-found brothers."[46]

In 1209 Francis decided the time had come to write a Rule—a governing document to solidify and codify his movement as a religious order. This meant, in turn, the time had likewise come for him to seek permission from the Holy See to exist according to their gospel conviction.

In the short document Francis composed in 1209 known as the "primitive Rule" (which has been lost), he articulated a literal application of Jesus's words in the Gospel to sell all possessions and serve the poor. The poor, for Francis, meant social outcasts and particularly lepers. At the time, the organizing principle of society was the Church with the pope at the center, from which emanated the various hierarchical levels of importance: around the pope would be cardinals, bishops, and other authorities; and after them would be clerics and laypeople. In the outermost level of significance would be the poor, the beggars, and—most pointedly, the lepers—destined to live out their days in isolation and beset by society's intolerance.

Francis's identity with lepers could have been seen as tantamount to a call to revolution in the Church, a concept noted succinctly by author Umberto Eco: "Every battle against heresy wants only to keep the leper as he is."[47] Francis's Rule and his blossoming movement reversed the Church's established *de facto* hierarchy, bringing the outcasts and the

---

44 Others, in name only, include Sabbatino, Morico, John of Capella, Philip the Long, John of Saint Constantia, Barbaro, Bernard Viridante, Silvestro, and Juniper.

45 *PC*,17,7; *CA:ED*, 193.

46 Julien of Speyer, *Life of Francis*, in *FA:ED*, vol. I, 380.

47 Umberto Eco, *The Name of the Rose*, trans. William Weaver (New York: Harcourt & Brace, 1983), 203.

lepers in from their isolation and placing them front and center in the family of God.

He and his small band set out for Rome to meet the pontiff, Pope Innocent III, whose name will come up again in this story. In those days heresies with a penitential bent were developing rapidly, and the Church was winnowing them out. Francis wanted papal approval so his infant order would be granted legitimacy and not deemed heretical or in violation of orthodox teachings. He was asking the Mother Church to affirm that his Rule was an authentic assertion of Christ's teaching. The only way he could gain credibility and the moral authority to teach was to win the approval of the sole governing authority of all things Christian— the pope.

At first Innocent III was not convinced by Francis's plea for approval and told Francis to go and pray.[48] Francis gained another hearing, and his request fueled squabbling in the papal Curia, Innocent's closest advisors and administrative leaders of the Church. Some felt his claims to poverty were too severe and would be impossible for any order to embrace in a sustainable way. Others in the Curia said his Rule smacked too much of heretics who made similar claims of renunciation, such as the Catharists and the Waldensians.[49] Francis replied that renunciation was a gift from Christ, so it did not depend upon man's abilities or weakness. "If the King of heaven promises his followers an eternal kingdom, he certainly will not let them go short of the material goods he bestows on good and bad without distinction."[50] He made it humbly but forcefully clear that he was simply asking that he and his fraternity be allowed to live out the gospel

---

48 *2C, FA:ED,* vol. 2, 254.

49 Catharists and Waldensians similarly embraced poverty, as Francis did, but denied the authority of the Roman Church, asserting that Jesus conferred on every individual authority as a "priesthood" (from the New Testament, I Peter 2). The Cathars also upheld the notion that the divine spark within every human being was corrupted by the flesh, thus concluding the material world was evil. Waldensian conviction was not altogether inconsistent with that of Francis. However, when the movement's founder, Peter Waldo, solicited permission to preach from Church authorities, he was refused. Nevertheless, he continued to preach without permission. Waldensians and Catharists were both deemed heretics.

50 Bonaventure, *Major Life,* in *Omnibus,* vol. I, 653.

freely as they understood it from Jesus himself—and that they be able to do so without interference from the Church.

After this second meeting with Francis, Innocent III had a dream in which he saw the Basilica of St. John Lateran—the cathedral in Rome that served as the official ecclesiastical seat of the pope—with towers creaking and walls cracking. He saw himself in the dream looking on helplessly as a small man dressed as a peasant, barefoot and with a rope about his waist, came toward the Lateran piazza and stood beside one of the crumbling walls and shouldered it until it stood erect. Innocent perceived the dream to be an omen. He became convinced that the little man who shouldered the falling palace was the mendicant peasant who had come asking for his blessing. Seeing Francis the next time, he embraced him and "granted his request unconditionally."[51] Innocent III orally approved Francis's first short Rule, known then as *Propositum vitae,* and thus the new Order of the Friars Minor ("lesser brothers") was born. Francis and his brothers received the tonsure—the shaved portion at the crown of the head that signaled the pope's permission to preach—and Francis went back to Assisi, where he "began to speak out more boldly owing to the apostolic authority he had been granted."[52]

The Mother Church could see, with this swiftly rising tide manifest in Francis Bernardone, that unless it somehow harnessed this force it would be vanquished by it. This set the stage for the explosion of the Franciscan movement. This movement, according to one early biographer, greatly benefitted the Church, especially because of Francis's "felicitous leadership of both sexes."[53] That brings us back to Clare.

---

51 Bonaventure, *Major Life,* 653.
52 Julien of Speyer, *Life of Francis, FA:ED,* vol. I, 385.
53 Julien of Speyer, *Life of Francis, FA:ED,* vol. I, 385.

CHAPTER 3

|||||||||||||||||||||||||||||||||||||||||||

TRAUMA

he early sources create a stunning, sometimes shocking, depiction of the dramatic events surrounding Clare's choice to leave her family and follow Francis. It was an event that sent tremors through Assisi at the time and its impact remains in force to this day. Everyone in town knew that Francis had scripted the drama, which Clare's blood sister Beatrice confirmed in the testimonies related to Clare's canonization: "[Francis] went to her many times, so that the virgin Clare acquiesced, renounced the world and all earthly things and went to serve God as soon as she was able." Another witness, a knight of Assisi named Ugolino di Pietro Girardone, said Francis's complicity in the episode "was public knowledge and known by everyone."[54]

These are the details of Clare's departure. The noblewomen of the house of Offreduccio attended Mass together on Palm Sunday sometime between the years 1210 and 1212.[55] Clare sat on the bench with her sisters and mother wearing elegant attire, as would befit a noblewoman on so festive a religious occasion.[56]

As was the tradition in that day, and remains so in many churches throughout the world today, on Palm Sunday worshipers rise from their

54 PC: CA:ED, 191.
55 It is uncertain which year Clare left her family home; some assert it took place in March of 1211, others March of 1212.
56 Palm Sunday, celebrated the week before Resurrection Sunday, highlighted the occasion of Jesus's final entrance into Jerusalem before his death, when crowds turned out to greet him with palm fronds.

seats to go to the altar and receive a palm frond, which they raise in memory of the grand entrance of Jesus into Jerusalem in the last week of his life. On this particular Palm Sunday, however, while Ortolana and two of her daughters advanced to the altar, the young Clare remained in her place weeping. The presiding Bishop Guido[57] took note of the disconsolate Clare alone on the bench, tear tracks on her delicate cheeks. Departing from church protocol, he left the platform and went to her to extend a branch, which she accepted. But the reason for her tears did not abate.

That was the night that she and Francis, with the assistance of Bishop Guido, had determined would be the moment of her flight. After dark, Clare cloaked herself to face the bracing night winds off Mount Subasio, loosened the iron bolt from a hidden door in the family home,[58] and slipped away from her childhood home and her life as she knew it, never to return.

"Embarking on her long-desired flight," as one source described it, Clare would have skirted through Assisi's dimly lit alleys to escape through the southern gate that opened to the plain below town, where Francis and a small contingent of brothers awaited her. Then, upon her arrival, "Francis took charge."[59]

His first act, now that Clare was under his care, was to cut her hair, or give her the tonsure. The tonsure is a dramatic and decisive symbol—a consecration, really—both for male and female penitents. It marks their intention to leave their lives in the world and embrace a new kind of life under a different set of rules. That Francis assumed the role of administering this consecration is a bold reminder of his sense of self-direction as he began to establish himself in his new vocation and his new order. Renowned medieval professor and Franciscan historian Marco

---

57 This is the same priest who had covered Francis's nakedness with his cloak a few years prior, when Francis made his dramatic break with his family. See *Mended*, 63–64.

58 This was known as the death door, that is, the door from which bodies of deceased family members would be removed from the home for burial.

59 Paschal Robinson, OSF, "St. Clare," *Franciscan Essays*, 31–49.

Bartoli, described the gesture this way: "Clare was not an ordinary young girl leaving her parents to enter monastic life. Nor was Francis a bishop—to whom the consecration of virgins was normally reserved. In fact, he was not even a priest but only a layman, and yet he took upon himself the right to consecrate Clare."[60] Protestant historian Paul Sabatier adds, "Francis was too much of an idealist to be prudent or to conform to any pretentious custom of good manners."[61]

Bartoli elsewhere presses the question: "After this liturgy, what had Clare become?" He makes the point that Clare had not undergone a novitiate, the period of training, preparation, and discernment that a member of a religious order undergoes prior to taking vows. So the tonsure could not have made Clare a nun. "Clare promised to observe no rule, she did not receive a monastic veil, she did not enter any settled, canonically erected community. . . . [T]he tonsure before the altar of Saint Mary of the Porziuncola was not a monastic consecration but a penitential gesture. Clare did not become a nun but a penitent, a *mulier religiosa,* a religious woman, a woman of penance."[62] And, just as Francis and his followers had become men of penance, Bartoli concludes, "They welcomed Clare as one of themselves."[63]

I mentioned in the Introduction that on the night Clare ran from her family home to follow Francis, her life would unfold in ways she never anticipated. From the start, almost instantly after the dramatic gesture of the tonsure at the altar, the terms of her decision began to change and she had to adapt. Aspects of her self-identity—both the one of nobility she left behind in remembrance and in the anticipation of the new one of poverty she was now forging—began to be stripped away like layers from an onion. The first layer was her abandoning a life of privilege as a marriageable noblewoman. This was exchanged for becoming, essentially,

60 Robinson, "St. Clare," 31–49.
61 Paul Sabatier, *Vie de saint François d'Assise* (Paris, 1926), 173.
62 *LCl* 8 *CA:ED* p. 287, says she received "the insignia of penance." See Padovese, Luigi, "Clare's Tonsure: Act of Consecration or Sign of Penance?" *GR* 6 (1992): 67–80.
63 M. Bartoli, *Saint Clare: Beyond the Legend,* trans. Sister Frances Teresa Downing, osc (Cincinnati: Franciscan Media, 2010), 58.

a beggar in beggar's clothing. She made this choice; it was not imposed upon her. Even so, no level of youthful idealism could have prepared her for the rough road that unfolded immediately upon her decisive break, especially after the cutting of her hair.

San Paolo delle Abbadesse

The tonsure signified that the brothers had received Clare as "one of themselves" and the life of such partnership and identity, particularly with Francis, is what she left everything to embrace. She wanted to follow Francis as his female companion and a feminine representation of his poverty and devotion. To that end, Francis promised her fealty; he would make sure she was protected and provided for as she settled into her new life as a religious penitent. But stark reality inevitably intruded upon this ideal, dictating that its particularities would have to be adapted. Clare could not abide with the brothers, even temporarily—that very night—without provoking rumors and potential scandal. Francis understood that temporary arrangements would have to be made for her residency until he completed his renovations at the small church of San Damiano. He knew as well that Clare would need to be housed in a place of sanctuary to defend her against the efforts of the family—who were knights, remember—and who inevitably would draw their swords to reclaim her. Francis knew the response from Clare's family would be visceral and confrontational. To offset the coming assault, he made the needed arrangements again with the aid and planning of Bishop Guido. (Francis could not have executed so daring a plot without special assistance from the local bishop.) He found her refuge that very night at a small Benedictine convent about five kilometers west of the Porziuncola, called San Paolo delle Abbadesse.

This important abbey, both nearby and well established, was the natural choice for a woman of rank to seek refuge. A few years before Clare's flight, Pope Innocent III delivered a bull granting certain papal privileges to the sisters there, including "receiv[ing] free women from secular life," and forbidding anyone to "molest this monastery."[64] This bull would have been rendered during the tenure of Bishop Guido, who would have made its sanctuary status known to Francis during the planning phase of this tumultuous event. It is likely that Guido enjoined the sisters there to receive Clare in the immediate aftermath of Clare's flight. Beyond that, the abbey was an optimal choice since a signature feature of Benedictine abbeys at the time was their setting up communities for wealthy female oblates seeking to embrace lives as religious.

Yet the Benedictines had a protocol for accepting such women, which included receiving a novice's dowry. This is how they financially sustained their respective convents. Clare, though a woman of rank, came that evening with no dowry to offer. She had already given away her dowry to the poor, in keeping with the model of Francis, who embodied the teaching and example of Jesus. This meant that Clare entered San Paolo not as a nun, but as a servant.[65] This status made the effrontery to the family all the more egregious. It was bad enough that she had defied the intention of the family to further their fortunes and influence through a profitable marriage of their highly prized and lovely eldest daughter. But to have such insouciance marked by such servitude was too much! She had chosen not to be a nun, but a *servant* of the nuns.

After a day or two of recovery, Clare's family did indeed track her down. And, as expected, they came with force to defend the honor of the family name. As it is written in the *Legend of Saint Clare:*

> But after the news reached her relatives, they condemned with a broken heart the deed and proposal of the virgin and, banding together as one, they ran to the place, attempting to obtain what they could not. They employed violent force, poisonous advice,

---

64 Fortini/Moak, 344. The bull, dated May 5, 1201, was directed to the "beloved daughters of Christ Sibilia, abbess of the monastery of San Paolo of Fonte Tiberino, and her sisters." The monastery was located along a last stretch of the Chiagio River, which flowed into the Tiber.

65 Bartoli has a good discussion of this in his book *Saint Clare: Beyond the Legend,* 60–63.

and flattering promises, persuading her to give up such a worthless deed that was unbecoming to her class and without precedent in her family.[66]

The original Latin of the phrase, "persuading her to give up such a worthless deed" reads: "*suadentes ab huiusmodi vilitate discedere.*" Historian Bartoli notes that such defiance was equivalent to "betraying her proper condition as an aristocrat." He adds, "[A] nobleman who behaved with *vitalis* was one who committed some sort of crime, who had not kept faith with his word, or who betrayed his origins."[67] Arnaldo Fortini explains it this way: "The violence of the reaction of Clare's family to this rebellious girl must be understood against the medieval concept of honour, in which criticism or infamy brought on by the deeds of any member of a family or clan was to be equally shared by all. What women did was to be an especial threat to the family honour."[68]

Clare responded with two dramatic and irrevocable gestures that made it impossible for her family to persist. She took hold of the altar cloths, which symbolized her claiming status as a protected refugee in the church and exempt from civil adjudication, and she revealed her tonsured hair, indicating an irreversible consecration. The *Legend* describes the scene:

Taking hold of the altar cloths, she bared her tonsured head, maintaining that she would in no way be torn away from the service of Christ. With the increasing violence of her relatives, her spirit grew and her love—provoked by injuries—provided strength. For many days, even though she endured an obstacle in the way of the Lord and her own [relatives] opposed her proposal of holiness, her spirit did not crumble and her fervor did not

66 *LegC, CA:ED,* 287.
67 Bartoli, *Saint Clare: Beyond the Legend,* 60.
68 Fortini/Moak, 345, note h.

diminish. Instead, amid words and deeds of hatred, she molded her spirit anew in hope.[69]

Seeing the tonsured head made it clear to the family that they had lost Clare. They turned and let her be. Fortini notes, "Under the circumstances, one might wonder why Clare's family left so abruptly. This monastery, it must be remembered, had been placed under the jurisdiction of the bishop of Assisi by a papal bull of 1198, which has also threatened with excommunication anyone who used violence on lands subject to the bishop. Also, the Benedictine monasteries for women, organized on the feudal pattern, had armed force at their disposal and were capable of making violators pay most dearly."[70]

Regardless of the family's ultimate acquiescence, the tumult they created unsettled the sisters at the abbey. First, it must be remembered that all this was occurring during the Church calendar's most sacred season—Holy Week, the days anticipating Jesus's death and resurrection. As was true of all religious communities during this very special week, the sisters at San Paolo had services, prayers, and other holy obligations to attend to. They took Clare in at the behest of Bishop Guido and in obedience to him. But circumstances quickly changed. Clare had come to them without a dowry and without the intention to join the Benedictine Order or acquiesce to the Benedictine Rule. This, in conjunction with the trouble brought upon them by so powerful a feudal family in Assisi, turned their hearts away from Clare and they pressed her to leave.

This put Francis in a bind. He was still finishing the second floor at the church of San Damiano (according to one historian I spoke with in Assisi[71]). He needed more time. Clare would have to be lodged elsewhere before she could take up residency at her long-awaited permanent dwelling.

---

69 *LegC* 5,9; *CA:ED,* 287.
70 Fortini/Moak, 345, note h.
71 Angela Seracchioli, pilgrim guide and author of *Di qui passò Francesco* (Terre di Mezzo, 2018).

Sant'Angelo di Panzo

How the small monastery called Sant'Angelo di Panzo came to be Clare's second landing spot is not known. One can only speculate. This remote monastery, tucked in a wooded area along the slope of Mount Subasio, was near where Francis frequently retreated to caves and the nearby hermitage. Even before Francis's conversion he would have had occasion to interact with the women living at Sant'Angelo since his father owned land in that area, and he frequently tended to his father's business on these lands. In any case, the women who were living there would have certainly known Francis, as everyone in and around Assisi knew him, and more so because of his frequent visits.

The setting was given the name Sant'Angelo for the archangel Michael, who, according to tradition, intervened on behalf of two warring brothers—both knights—who were living there and were locked in mortal combat over division of their deceased father's goods. The story goes that the brothers were each poised to deliver to the other the decisive fatal blow when the archangel appeared before them shining brightly. They dropped to their knees in obeisance to the holy messenger, and Michael, in turn, commanded them to render each other the kiss of peace. Upon doing so, the angel disappeared, and the two knights converted their mountainside castle to a monastery, naming it for the angel who saved them.

There is a lack of consensus about which women penitents were living there at the time when Clare arrived. Some assert Sant'Angelo—like San Paolo—was inhabited by Benedictine sisters; others maintain that the women who were living there belonged to an unaffiliated sect of women penitents known as Beguines. Little can be determined about what religious order, if any, these women belonged to. The default assumption seems to fall toward the Benedictines, given the pervasive presence of Benedictine women's convents throughout the region, as well as the abundance of Benedictine real estate. Historian Angela Seracchioli departs from this theory, asserting instead that at the time when Clare arrived, the property was inhabited by religious women who identified with the Beguines, a religious conglomerate of women who left their privileged lives to embrace the teachings of Jesus and live for the poor. Beguines remained unaffiliated because of their underlying belief that the apparatus of the Church was not needed in order for a believing woman to have access to God and to live the penitential life.

The movement started in northern Europe in the late twelfth century and lasted through the sixteenth, propelled by a gender imbalance created by incessant wars, plagues, and sometimes famine. Men were in short supply and marriageable women were in abundance. This created the conditions whereby "out of necessity, a new role and lifestyle emerged for unmarried women who were willing to work honestly and live pious lives."[72] *Beguines*, or "holy women," lived together communally, dedicating themselves to God, prayer, and good works, though they did not take vows or belong to the hierarchy of the Catholic Church. At the time when Clare arrived at Sant'Angelo, the movement had spread into points south, including the Italian peninsula. We have already seen how decisively Clare had rebuffed the idea of becoming a Benedictine nun, and her experience at San Paolo put an end to any further discussion on that point. It is unlikely that Francis would have subjected her to a similar trial by setting her up at another Benedictine convent. So it is not a stretch of reason or evidence to consider that, for this second stop on Clare's early pilgrimage, she found herself in the midst of Beguines.[73]

Whether among Beguines or Benedictines, from the start this new setting did not sit well with Clare. She had already experienced the shock and trauma of leaving her family home so decisively and enduring the raucous response of her family at San Paolo. Then, as a result of the family tumult, she bore the additional indignity of being expelled from San Paolo. It cannot be known whether this turn of events took Francis

72 "Beguines and Beghard," Wikipedia, https://en.wikipedia.org/wiki/Beguines_and_Beghards.
73 Seracchioli notes, "The Beguines at Sant'Angelo were nearer to Francis [in religious expression] than the Benedictines." Interview, November 4, 2018.

and Clare by surprise. Regardless, the situation left Francis scrambling. Again, Bishop Guido would have stepped in to sort things out. And upon leaving San Paolo, Clare was promptly relocated to the mountain setting of Sant'Angelo di Panzo, on the slope of Mount Subasio.

Here too, however, Clare was unhappy and in a state of distress. She was desperately lonely, and "her mind was not completely at peace."[74] To his credit, Francis tried to help. Clare needed him more viscerally than he was able to accommodate during this time, but he visited when he could and always brought a few of his brothers with him. Fortini says Clare "found herself plunged into bitter loneliness and thought with burning homesickness about Catherine, her favorite sister, her long-time confidante in everything."[75] As part of his attempt to help settle Clare, Francis arranged for Catherine to join her at Sant'Angelo. It was a good thought. And it elevated Clare's mood. But, predictably, this plan too would be met with more turmoil and family violence.

Clare's sister Catherine (to whom Francis would later give the name Agnes) was a few years younger than Clare, and the two had been close throughout their childhood. It is not known if, in the period prior to Clare's departure, they had plotted for Catherine to join her once Clare was settled. It certainly was not news to Catherine when the family discovered Clare had left. Whatever the plan may have been, it could not have included the hike up the slope of Mount Subasio to Sant'Angelo, since this arrangement was clearly abruptly and hastily contrived. Regardless, within a few days of Clare's arrival, which would have been mid-April by this point, Catherine made the trek up the snowy slope to take up residency with her beloved sister. As noted in the *Legend of Saint Clare*, "The divine majesty quickly gave her that first gift she so eagerly

---

74 *LCl, 9; CA:ED,* 287.
75 Fortini/Moak, 348.

sought"—her sister. "Embracing her with joy, [Clare] said, 'I thank God, most sweet sister, that he has heard my concern for you.' "[76]

The *Legend* describes the tumult that ensued:

> The next day, hearing Agnes [Catherine] had gone off to Clare, twelve men, burning with anger and hiding outwardly their evil intent, ran to the place and pretended to make peaceful entrance. They turned to Agnes, since they had long ago lost hope of reclaiming Clare, and said, "Why have you come to this place? Get ready to return immediately." When she responded that she did not want to leave her sister Clare, one of the knights, without sparing blows and kicks, tried to drag her away by her hair, while the others pushed her and lifted her in their arms.[77]

According to the *Legend,* they carried Catherine along the slope of the mountain, still tearing her clothes and pulling out her hair, casting them aside along the path. Clare followed them, imploring them on her sister's behalf. She at last found her sister near death on the ground alongside the road. How (and if) Clare convinced them to leave her is not known.[78] But no one knows how long she took to recover after being left along the road. In time, however, Francis tonsured Catherine, too, and gave her the new name of Agnes, for God's lamb (the Latin *agnus* means "lamb").

Lingering Questions

Apart from the trauma of Clare's flight from her family, one of the most contentious unresolved details related to this incident is the matter of her age at this time. It is a question made more confusing by the vague

---

76 *LCl*, 16, 24; *CA:ED*, 303.

77 *LCl*, 16, 25; *CA:ED*, 303.

78 The release of Catherine after her family's attempted retrieval is the first miracle associated with Clare. According to tradition, as the family members attempted to carry Catherine by force to take her back home, her body became so heavy as to be immovable and they were unable to move her. So they left her by the side of the road, near death.

and inconsistent accounts afforded by her canonization witnesses. Clare's age is generally contentious because there is no record of the date of her birth, and it is widely assumed that she was much younger than Francis, so their friendship could comfortably be defined only as that of a father and daughter. Nevertheless, the consensus of the witnesses suggests that Clare may have been older than was widely accepted at the time she left home to join Francis. Moreover, it indicates that her age was a subject that was talked about within the convent.

The answer is anything but clear. Clare was minimally in her late teens and possibly older. But, according to the witnesses in the process of her canonization, this much is known: She left to join Francis "as soon as she could." She fled the night of Palm Sunday in secret and alone. She did so at the behest of Francis, who met her and cut her hair. He had made all necessary arrangements for temporary asylum. Upon discovering her disappearance, the family reacted with force, trying and failing to retrieve her. The episode was big news in town and more so because Clare's shocking behavior had been scripted by the Bernardone boy, that one-time profligate-turned-lunatic friar. Clare's sister Catherine/Agnes nearly died at the hands of relatives, but didn't. And she lived out her days as a key member of what was to become Clare's Order of Franciscan women.

The implications are many. Bishop Guido perceived Clare's emotions as she wept alone on the bench that Palm Sunday, and he broke protocol to approach and encourage her. This suggests that he understood the cause of her tears. He and Francis were known to have shared a close bond, and Guido had been intimately involved with all previous critical decisions relating to Francis's religious life. Since Francis deemed him the "guardian and protector of souls," it is unlikely that Francis and Clare would have executed so daring a plan without consulting the bishop. It is also probable that the complicated logistics of Clare's temporary lodging would have required his helpful intervention. In any case, that day as she sat by herself on the bench, Bishop Guido gave Clare his blessing. It can also be inferred that Catherine/Agnes had been privy to the plan—

and probably knew that she would follow her sister shortly thereafter. Catherine kept track of Clare after the latter's departure and knew precisely where to go (to Clare's second location at Sant'Angelo di Panzo). She also no doubt anticipated the ruckus it would cause when the time came for her to join her.

Clare desired her flight "for a long time," which suggests that plans had been in the making for a lengthy period before the event. She fled "as soon as she was able," which likewise suggests something precluded her going sooner. We have already noted that Francis worked on San Damiano early on after his conversion, with the intention of housing women there (before he thought to begin an order). Yet the church belonged to the Benedictines, and rebuilt by him or not, he had to secure the arrangement to rent it permanently, which may have complicated the timing. We now know that for a long time—probably years—before Clare's departure, Francis was "admonishing" her and "whispering in her ears of a sweet espousal with Christ," encouraging her to follow him. In the end, Francis chose the day she would flee and where she would go while she "committed herself thoroughly to the counsel of Francis, placing him, after God, as the guide of her journey."[79]

So, "trembling with fear at the allurements of the flesh," she ran that night to join Francis, binding herself to his destiny and putting her life in his hands. He ultimately secured her lodging at San Damiano and "saw flourish inside a temple of the Spirit and outside, the work of his hands," wrote the early biographer Henri d'Avranches. Thus, the writer concluded, Francis "brought his plan to a happy end."

79 *LCl*, 3; *CA:ED*, 285.

CHAPTER 4

|||||||||||||||||||||||||||||||||||||||||

CONCESSIONS

otwithstanding the shock, trauma, and general disorientation that defined Clare's earliest days after following Francis, the real adjustments set in once she was safely ensconced at her permanent home at San Damiano. The *Legend* introduces this transition with two telling statements. The first: "She no longer wavered due to further changes of place"; the second: "She did not hesitate because of its smallness, nor did she fear its isolation. . . . Here she imprisoned her body for as long as it would live hiding it from the turmoil of the world."[80]

The first statement suggests, perhaps inadvertently, that during the tumultuous early days and weeks of her new life, Clare wavered. The Latin term used in this translation is *fluctuat*; she fluctuated, or (translated elsewhere) she "was tossed to and fro." Who can blame her? She was wrestling with the "capital choice [she had made] with no way back," as Seracchioli put it. The unforeseeable consequences were set in motion almost immediately after her break with the family at so young and impressionable an age. From the start she was forced to make mental adjustments to changing circumstances, as she would throughout her life as a radical religious. That she wavered is not surprising. What is telling is that, despite her doubts, she stayed the course.

80 *LCl*, 5; *CA:ED*, 288.

The latter statement goes further in demonstrating how Clare's initial design in leaving her life as a noble to become a "Poor Sister"[81] was at some point radically reconfigured. The notion that "here she imprisoned her body for as long as [she] would live" was completely alien to her thoughts and plans in the early years of her religious life at San Damiano. Yes, her new home was small and isolated, located to the south of the center of Assisi, below the town walls. And yes, there was not much going on there, and Clare, like her mother, was a woman of action. Yet she was happy to be settled in the place that carried so profound an impact on Francis's life, the place he rebuilt with his hands specifically *for her*. Even so, when she went bounding toward her new life with Francis, she saw herself embracing the same kind of life that he had adopted, and her tonsure marked her as one of his band of mendicants.[82] She waited and hoped that, once her living situation stabilized, she could live out the Franciscan ideal alongside Francis.

Their Courtly Ideal

A critical element that both Francis and Clare brought to their bold new religious enterprise was the concept of chivalry, a romantic notion that flourished in the Middle Ages. It shaped knightly aspirations, male and female bonds, and religious devotion. Fueled by the legend of King Arthur—his knights of the Round Table, and his devotion to his

---

81 As will be discussed in more detail in due course, Clare fought strenuously to retain the moniker for her Order as the "Poor Sisters" over the term "Enclosed Nuns," a term that was continually being foisted upon her by church authorities. "Poor Sisters" hearkens Francis's denotation of his Order as the "Friars Minor" (or "Poor Brothers"). Clare's term for the women paralleled Francis's term for the men. I interviewed Pietro Maranesi, a Friars Minor Capuchin, the author of the book *La Clausura di Chiara d'Assisi* (Perugia, IT: Edizioni Porziuncola, 2012), who forcefully argues that enclosure, for Clare, was at best a secondary matter. She preferred her order to be known as "poor sisters," highlighting their unity in poverty, rather than as "enclosed nuns." Personal interview, November 8, 2018, Assisi, Italy.

82 Francis's followers referred to themselves as "mendicants." Mendicants (Latin *mendicare*, "to beg") were members of religious orders in the Roman Catholic Church who took a vow of poverty, renouncing personal and communal property. The term evolved to describe those in the penitential movement who went from place to place to preach.

lady, Queen Guinevere—courtly love (*amour courtois*) was glorified in the poetry of the twelfth-century French troubadours, who Francis idealized and emulated in his youth.[83] Courtly love marked a revolution in attitudes about sexuality, as the lady was cherished as a poetic and personal inspiration and no longer reduced to a disposable pawn in the manipulation of arranged marriages. This held great appeal, especially to women of rank, and Clare would have been well-versed in courtly ideals. "[T]he romances of chivalry were told in every feudal household. The romantic temperament was her own, and tales of high adventure and deathless loyalty would be sweet to her ears."[84]

In his pre-conversion youth, Francis aspired to knighthood and the culture of knighthood both in war and carnal pursuit of women.[85] After his conversion and in the context of his blossoming relationship with Clare, Francis integrated the same knightly and courtly ideals into the fabric of his religious devotion. He called his brothers his "knights of the Round Table."[86] Beyond that, Francis "brought the spirit of romantic chivalry into man's relations with his God . . . [and] consecrated the emotion and ideal of chivalry into veritable sacraments of the life in Christ . . . Clare lived in the vision of this religious chivalry: she drank in its truth and beauty with quick appreciation, and held to it with passionate loyalty."[87]

In keeping with this model, when Clare abandoned her life of privilege and security as a noblewoman, Francis bound himself to her welfare, assuring her of his devotion to protect and provide for her. To that end,

---

83 "Writing in the second half of the twelfth century, Chrétien de Troyes was the inventor of Arthurian literature drawing from material circulated by itinerant Breton minstrels and legitimized by Geoffrey of Monmouth's pseudo-historical *Historia Regum Britanniae* (*History of the Kings of Britain*, c. 1136–37). Chrétien fashioned a new form known today as courtly romance." Chrétien de Troyes, *Arthurian Romances*, trans. with intro. and notes by William W. Kibler (New York: Penguin, 1991), 222–23.

84 Cuthbert, *The Romanticism of Saint Francis*, 83.

85 *Mended*, chapter 2, 19ff.

86 *MP,* 72; *FA:ED,* vol. 2, 208.

87 *MP,* 72; *FA:ED,* vol. 2, Cuthbert, 80.

as Clare noted in the *Form of Life*, which she wrote near the end of her life, Francis had given her written assurance that he would care for her. She quoted his words:

> According to the inspiration you did take, daughters and servants of the Most High King, the heavenly Father and the Holy Spirit, you promised choosing to live according to the perfection of the Holy Gospel. I will promise for myself and my brothers will always have you as very special care and concern.[88]

Jaques de Vitry

One of the earliest sources offering a glimpse into how this ideal unfolded for Clare's new life—and for the women who would join her—comes from the French Cardinal Jacques de Vitry (1170–1240). A contemporary of Francis and Clare, after having held the position of Bishop of Acre for twelve years, he took the honored seat of Cardinal Bishop of Tusculum,[89] near Rome, in 1228. During his career he made numerous ventures throughout the Middle East and Europe as an observer and interpreter of flowering religious lay movements, which he documented in his seminal work *Historia orientalis et occidentalis*.[90] He was particularly interested in women's religious movements and wrote another major work highlighting the life and work of a leading figure in the Beguine movement, Marie d'Oignies.[91] In 1216, when Clare would

---

88 *LCl*, 6; *CA:ED*, 117–18.

89 The Diocese of Frascati (Lat.: Tusculana) is a suburbicarian see of the Holy Roman Church and a diocese of the Catholic Church in Italy, based at Frascati, near Rome. The bishop of Frascati is a Cardinal Bishop; from the Latin name of the area, the bishop has also been called Bishop of Tusculum. Tusculum was destroyed in 1191. The bishopric moved from Tusculum to Frascati, a nearby town which is first mentioned in the pontificate of Pope Leo IV. Until 1962, the Cardinal-Bishop was concurrently the diocesan bishop of the see in addition to any curial duties he possessed. Pope John XXIII removed the Cardinal Bishops from any actual responsibility in their suburbicarian dioceses and made the title purely honorific.

90 *Historia orientalis et occidentalis* "devotes considerable attention to the religious movements present in Western Europe at the time and describes in particular his impressions of the Beguines, the Humiliati, and the Lesser Brothers and Sisters." *CA:ED*, 427.

91 Jacques de Vitry, *De Maria Oigneacensi in Namurcensi Belgii Diocesi*, ed. (contd.)

have been living as a Poor Sister for approximately four years, he visited Assisi and was enamored of the model of religious devotion among the Franciscans he encountered there, both male and female. He described his impressions in a letter written from Genoa in October 1216 to a friend in Liège, Belgium. His mention of the Franciscans is worth quoting in its entirety:

> I found one consolation in those parts, nevertheless: many men and women, rich and worldly, after renouncing everything for Christ, fled the world. They are called Lesser Brothers and Lesser Sisters. They are held in great esteem by the Lord Pope and the cardinals. They do not occupy themselves with temporal affairs, but work each day with great desire and enthusiastic zeal to capture those souls that were perishing from the vanities of the world and to bring them along with them. . . . They live according to the form of the primitive Church of which it is written 'The multitude of believers was of one heart and one soul . . . .' They go into the cities and villages during the day, so that they convert others, giving themselves to active work; but they return to their hermitages or solitary places at night, employing themselves in contemplation.
>
> The women live near the cities in various hospices. They accept nothing, but live from the work of their hands. In fact, they are very much offended and disturbed because they are honored by the clergy and laity more than they deserve.[92]

De Vitry's description draws a picture of the lives of the Poor Sisters as active and engaged and interacting with members of the local community

---

D. Paperbroec, *Acta Sanctorum*, June 5 (Paris 1867): 542–72; English translation: *The Life of Marie d'Oignies*, trans. Margo H. King (Saskatoon, Saskatchewan: Peregrina Publishing Co., 1986).

92 The reference to "hospices" means "simple poor houses that became dwelling places for many of the new religious movements of women." Jacques de Vitry document cited in *CA:ED*, 428.

and then retreating to their convents and hermitages in the evenings for prayer and solitude. It is a picture consistent with the kind of life Clare envisioned when she traipsed through the field grass the night she left her family home to follow Francis. A wide swath of Franciscan scholars and researchers concur that the testimony of de Vitry strongly suggests that the Poor Sisters indeed lived a mendicant, active existence in concert with the Brothers. This was the picture of religious life that both Francis and Clare envisioned and attempted to embody in the early days of their religious vocation.[93]

As they hammered out the terms of this revolutionary enterprise, Francis, in any case, deemed Clare the lady of the castle. Thus, true to the code of chivalry, he reiterated his devotion near the end of his life when he wrote: "I desire and promise you personally and in the name of my friars, that I will always have the same loving care and special solicitude for you as for them."[94] This promise, in time, would prove contentious for all parties. But in that moment, it was his intent to order the lives of his female members through the honored mutuality that befits the code of chivalry.

De Vitry made his observations in 1216. Around that same time, pressure was being put upon Clare from two fronts that would result in a change in this picture and in her way of life. The first was her friend and guardian of the Franciscans, Bishop Ugolino dei Segni of Ostia—later Pope Gregory IX. And the second, oddly, would become Francis.

Bishop Ugolino/Pope Gregory IX

Ugolino dei Segni (c. 1170–1241) emerges among the panoply of players in Clare's story as equal parts astonishingly devoted defender of

---

93 Catharine Mooney, "The 'Lesser Sisters' in Jacques de Vitry's 1216 Letter," *Franciscan Studies*, Vol. 69 (2011), 1–29. She adds, "[de Vitry's] letter has been used to argue further that the women explicitly grouped together with the Lesser Brothers, were known by the parallel title of the 'Lesser Sisters,' who enjoyed freedom to come and go as they wished during these early years." Other scholars demur, however, arguing that de Vitry's reference is too general to conclude definitively that this was the case for Clare and the sisters at San Damiano.

94 "Canticle of Exhortation to Saint Clare and Her Sisters," *CA:ED*, 393.

the penitential movement, and stunningly pragmatic arbiter. He was a superstar, as medieval characters go, and wielded extraordinary influence in the personal and religious lives of both Francis and Clare.

One might consider him a pre-Renaissance renaissance man. He was born of the same illustrious Segni family as Pope Innocent III (his uncle), the same Pope who approved Francis's Rule in 1209 that officially established the Order of the Friars Minor. Like his uncle, Ugolino studied theology in Paris and law in Bologna and early in his career showed himself astute and judicious when it came to ecclesiastical law and international diplomacy. So his uncle, Pope Innocent III, advanced him. Innocent too had been a superstar. By the time Francis and his small following had come to him requesting validation (in 1209) the young pope had established dominion over most of central and southern Italy and had secured the Holy See as the political seat of John, king of England; Pietro II, king of Aragon; Kaloyan, king of Bulgaria; Ottokar, king of Bohemia; Alphonso IX, king of León (in Spain); and several Cilician kingdoms of Armenia.

Recognizing his nephew's instincts as a diplomat and ecclesiastical enthusiast, Innocent invoked Ugolino's aid in navigating the tenuous and disturbed waters of medieval political and ecclesiastical symbiosis. In 1206 Innocent promoted him to the cardinal bishopric of Ostia (a port city of Rome), a position he held until he was made pope in 1227. During the pontificate of his uncle's successor, Pope Honorius III (1216–27), Ugolino continued to play a leading role on many fronts, garnering the trust and goodwill of both the pope and another key player who would emerge later in Clare's story: the youthful emperor-elect Frederick II, king of Sicily. Frederick, in time, would become Gregory's greatest antagonist.

Innocent III had been tolerant of penitential movements. He understood the advantage of bringing these reformers under the auspices of the Church and, to that end, he was willing to concede certain points— their commitment to live in poverty, for example—in exchange for a profession of allegiance to the Church. Under Innocent's guidance, both the Franciscans and the Dominicans were born. But it was Ugolino (later,

Pope Gregory IX) who helped these one-time flailing movements gain ballast enough to grow, thrive, and establish themselves as a major force in Church reform. Ugolino was a deeply spiritual man and he supported the penitential movements, particularly the Franciscans.

Beyond friendship with Francis, Ugolino served as cardinal-protector of the Franciscan Order at Francis's request, and he was also a personal and affectionate adviser to Clare as she angled to give shape to the female arm, which she insisted upon calling the Poor Sisters.[95] It was Ugolino's help that ultimately enabled these movements to rise above sundry other penitential movements that, in due course, would disappear or be otherwise assimilated.

Such legitimacy was not realized without certain reciprocal concessions that the reformers would likewise have to render. The evolution of Clare's situation and the concessions she was forced to make are evidenced in a variety of sources, including her writings, testimonies of those who knew her, and papal documents. These sources reflect the pressure she faced, particularly as the institution of the Church, inch by inch, imposed a strict delineation for how this female Order would arrange itself.

Innocent III—Privilege of Poverty

All seemed on track when the first ruling came from Innocent III in 1215 or 1216 in a bull titled *Privilegium pauperitatis*. In this document he allowed the sisters of San Damiano the privilege to live without an assured income or ownership of property, in keeping with the model Francis upheld for his Order.[96] In part, his ruling read:

[Y]ou propose to have no possessions in any way, wanting to follow the footsteps in everything of the One who for us made himself

95 They would later be called the Poor Clares.
96 Clare petitioned Innocent III for the "privilege" of absolute poverty, not merely for the individual members but for the community as a whole. "Highly pleased with the unusual request he granted it," says the saint's biographer, with his own hand "cum hilaritate magna" ("Röm. Quartalschrift," 1902, 97; see also Robinson, "Life of Saint Clare," note 114).

poor, thus becoming the way, the truth, and the life. And you are not frightened by the lack of necessary things in this intention, so long as the right hand of your celestial Spouse is under your head to support the weakness of your body, which you have disciplined to be subordinate to the rule of your will. After all, he who feeds the birds of the air and clothes the lilies of the field will not fail you in both food and clothing. . . . And, therefore, as you have asked, we with apostolic favour approve your aim of highest poverty, granting, with the authority of this writing, that by no one may you be forced to receive possessions. . . .[97]

Innocent enabled Clare to launch "an entirely new form of convent community, which maintains itself on alms and the profits of manual labor in the same way as the [male] Franciscans."[98] Also embedded in this arrangement was the implicit role of the male brothers to aid the sisters in their lives' sustenance. So, while Innocent affirmed Clare's insistence that the female Franciscans be permitted to abide without the security of property and possessions, nevertheless, they did have a degree of dependence upon the friars to aid them, something that would become troublesome in the coming years as each arm of the Order grew.

Francis Makes Her Abbess

Even at this early stage, more women were joining Clare at San Damiano and others were establishing small female monasteries in nearby locales. Francis's following was likewise swelling to surprising numbers, and he began to recognize the need to bring order to the chaos. Francis was an astonishing figure in many ways, but one way he was not astonishing was as an administrator. Inevitably, when the numbers increased, the Order's operations had to be managed. And managing

97 Fortini/Moak, 360–61.
98 Bolton, Brenda. *"Mulieres Sanctae," Women in Medieval Society*, ed. Brenda Bolton (Philadelphia: University of Pennsylvania Press, 1976), 285.

things was not Francis's forte. As part of his effort to harness the growth of his unwieldy movement, he enjoined Clare to take charge of the women and bring the community at San Damiano under greater discipline. To that end, he asked her to assume the role of abbess—something Clare very much did *not* want to do. Sister Pacifica dei Guelfucci, a witness on the *Process of Canonization* and Clare's childhood friend, described the intensity of her resistance: "[T]hree years after Lady Clare had been in the Order, at the prayers and insistence of Saint Francis, who almost forced her, she accepted the direction and government of the sisters."[99]

The role of abbess in the Middle Ages was one of power—"They granted and withdrew benefices, took part in councils and called synods; in many dual cloisters *they* exercised authority. Often, like the abbot, they had the jurisdiction of a bishop without full powers of consecration. This meant that they exercised temporal and spiritual power in their realm just as the bishop did in his diocese. The liturgical sources and rites of consecration show that abbesses often received the staff and miter and thus full teaching and jurisdictional authority."[100] The idea of possessing and wielding such power repulsed Clare, and she fiercely resisted Francis's request. Some have suggested that her reason for resisting was out of a sense of unworthiness in assuming so authoritative a role in the early years of her life at San Damiano. Others maintain, as I do, that Clare's resistance was not fueled by humility but by a recognition that, once her life and those of the sisters at San Damiano was so ordered, she would lose the freedom as a mendicant that she had so hoped to realize. Becoming abbess meant overseeing the lives of the sisters *in situ*, while *de facto* suggesting a more sedentary—even cloistered—way of life.[101]

The situation was evolving; her circumstances were changing. Francis was asking her to assume this role—no, he was *insisting upon* it—and

---

99 *PC*, I, 6; *CA:ED*, 146.

100 A. Valerio, "Women in the 'Societas Christiana': 10th-12th centuries." *TD* 33:1 (Spring, 1986), 156.

101 This is the view also held by Clarian scholar Chiara Frugoni in *Una solitudine abitata: Chiara d'Assisi* (Roma: Laterza, 2006).

she was bound by obedience. Just as she wavered during those first tumultuous weeks of her new life but did not give up, here again she was confronted with terms she had not anticipated. Against her wishes, she accepted the role, and her thoughts, of necessity, turned to organizing the lives of her sisters and undertaking the consolidation of the female Franciscan Order.

Even in this role, however, Clare forged her own path and established her own rules. Eschewing the authority of power that came with the role, she saw her role as abbess as more pastoral than judicial. She described in her *Form of Life* (1253): "The sisters are bound to observe the canonical form in the election of the abbess [that is, the sisters choose their abbess; she would not be appointed]. . . . Let her also strive to preside over the others more by her virtue and holy behavior than by her office, so that, moved by her example, the sisters may obey her more out of love than out of fear."[102]

Fourth Lateran Council

In the meantime, reforming impulses among various penitential groups continued to assert themselves, and the numbers swelled. The disparate nature of this movement carried the potential to wreak chaos on Mother Church. As a result, the Fourth Lateran Council[103] declared that no new religious orders could be formed and that any reform movement wanting legitimacy would have to subscribe to the governing Rule of an already-existing Rule:

The founding of new religious orders is forbidden. New monasteries must accept a rule already approved. A monk may

---

102 *FLCl* 3; *CA:ED*, 114.
103 The Lateran Councils were ecumenical gatherings (of which there were five) of the Roman Church held in the Lateran Palace in Rome between the years 1123 and 1517. The fourth Lateran Council (1215), which directly affected Clare's situation, was considered the greatest ecumenical council before the Council of Trent. It was called by Innocent III, and more than 400 bishops, 800 abbots and priors, envoys of many European kings, and personal representatives of Frederick II took part. The purpose of the council was twofold: to strategize for the reforming of the church and the recovery of the Holy Land.

not reside in different monasteries nor may one abbot preside over several monasteries.

Both Francis—who had already secured the approval of a primitive Rule—and Clare, operating from Francis's example, would in time feel the pinch of this dictum. But before this happened, Francis made a decision that would change everything and even initiate the beginning of the end of his movement as he configured it. Despite the wrangling within the ranks of his burgeoning Order, at his heart Francis was a mendicant who had news to share and he would not be dissuaded from that mission.

In 1219 he left the Italian peninsula to join the Fifth Crusade in Damietta, the northern Egyptian port city in the Nile delta. This episode embodies all the drama and improbability that marked his transformation from a knight of arms to a knight of the gospel. It forged for Francis and for others, by his example, a new paradigm for engaging an enemy in the context of a bloody war that was at its heart religious. It also removed him from direct oversight of Clare and the Poor Sisters and left his changing Order without their captain.

Francis was determined to engage the leader of the Muslim army in the name of Christ and would not be denied his intention to go, even if it meant death—as all of his companions deemed it would. In early summer 1219, he and a small contingent of brothers said goodbye to their beloved Assisi. Those to whom he bade farewell believed they would not see Francis again in this life.

The result of this expedition was an improbable visit with Muslim Sultan Malik al-Kamil that remains one of the most astonishing encounters in religious history.[104] It is not known how much time he spent with the Sultan, or any travels he may have embarked upon subsequently. Regardless, Francis was compelled to return to Italy abruptly in the summer of 1220, after one of his brothers, Stefano, tracked him down all the way from Italy to report troubling news. It seemed that some of the

104 For a detailed account of this fascinating visit, see *Mended*, 109.

brothers back home presumed Francis dead and had thus taken it upon themselves to change things within the Order. Stefano explained that an all-out revolt was occurring in Assisi, and it seemed less a rejection of Francis's ideals than a rejection of Francis himself.

So Francis and his companions began their return journey. Upon his return, Francis would find himself caught in a spiral of conflict, isolation, and suffering that would carry him to his end.

Returning to Assisi, he found the movement in turmoil and was alarmed to discover that some had tried to impose an outside governing apparatus on the Poor Sisters—an arrangement based upon the Rule of Saint Benedict.

Ugolino's Form of Life (1219)

The issues highlighted at the Fourth Lateran Council of 1215 provoked a new resolve on the part of the Curia to become more heavy-handed about the organization of women's orders. Innocent III's successor, Pope Honorius III, a few years later undertook consolidating the female religious orders under a single model harkening the Benedictine model for religious women's societies. Benedictine women were protected and granted real estate and the benefits of the endowments (dowries) brought to the Order by their families. These women lived out their days in industry and prayer without the burdens or distractions of having to make their own way or pay their own bills.

To this end, Honorius III, through his friend Bishop Ugolino, issued an updated "Manner of Life" for the Poor Clares in 1219 during the time when Francis was away. Three changes were obvious. The first was Ugolino's using the phrase "Enclosed [cloistered] Nuns" instead of Poor Sisters: "Therefore, beloved daughters in Christ, agreeing in a grateful spirit with your just requests, we have decided to incorporate in this letter the *Form and Manner of Living* which we delivered to all the Poor Cloistered Nuns."[105]

105 *CA:ED*, 75.

Another change came in the body of the document, outlining the way these women's monasteries were to live:

> So that the order of your life, firmly built and established on Christ after the manner of and in imitation of those who have served the Lord without complaint and have crowned the beginning of their blessed and holy way of life with the most blessed conclusion of perseverance, may be able to grow into a holy temple in the Lord and by following the footsteps of the saints may be able to reach the reward of such a high vocation directly and happily, we give you the *Rule of Saint Benedict* to be observed in all things which are in no way contrary to that same *Form of Life* that was given to you by us and by which you have especially chosen to live. This *Rule of Saint Benedict* is known to embody the perfection of virtue and the greatest discretion.

Finally, Ugolino's document stated this: "Therefore, after abandoning and despising the vanity of the world, it is proper and becoming [for] all who have resolved to embrace and hold to your religion to observe this law of life and discipline, and *remain enclosed* the whole time of their life. After they have entered the enclosure of this religion and have assumed the religious habit, *they should never be granted any permission or faculty to leave [this enclosure]*, unless perhaps some are transferred to another place to plant or build up this same religion."

While Benedict's Rule on one level involved a vow of poverty, in Clare's case, the idea of poverty was understood in differing degrees. Many women of rank and wealth were drawn to these penitential women's societies and to that end left their families and social standing to embrace a life of devotion and, yes, poverty. This was a poverty that stood in contrast to the privileged lives they had renounced. Yet, even in this newly embraced poverty they enjoyed a degree of security; "Monastic women willingly accepted land grants and tax exemptions given them by wealthy relatives and solicitous popes."[106]

In contrast, Clare, following Francis, wanted to live under "the privilege of poverty" in a way that exactly mimicked the life of our Lord and obeyed his command, as Francis dictated in his first "primitive Rule," the short document he composed in 1209 for approval by the pope. The mandate of his first Rule articulated a literal application of Jesus's words in the Gospel to sell all possessions and serve the poor. Francis reiterated this mandate in his note to Clare, after she joined him "to live according to the perfection of the Holy Gospel." Neither of them wanted the "security" of endowments or dowries.

All along in his short journey as founder of this new Order, Francis had made it humbly but forcefully clear that he was simply asking of the Church authorities that he and his fraternity (and sorority) be allowed to live the Gospel as they understood it from Jesus himself—and that they be able to do so without interference. This was the line that had been drawn: Francis and Clare's "privilege of poverty" in strict conformity to the words of Jesus versus Mother Church's efforts to bring women's orders under the model of the Benedictine Rule, which allowed for the security of land and property ownership.

Benedict's Rule, which in Francis's absence had been imposed upon the Poor Sisters in all their locations, allowed for ownership of property and other privileges and protections. These changes were an affront to Clare, and she fiercely resisted appropriating them at San Damiano. When Francis learned of it, he too was outraged, as this new model violated their unyielding convictions about poverty. Francis learned that this new policy had been imposed upon all the satellite convents of the Poor Sisters, with the sole exception being Clare's dominion at

---

106 Joan Mueller, *The Privilege of Poverty* (University Park, PA: Pennsylvania State University Press, 2006), 2.

San Damiano—a testament to her stubborn tenacity to remain true to Francis's ideals. Upon his return, Francis forcefully reprimanded the overseer who had attempted these changes for the Poor Sisters, a scenario that portended a conflict that would define Clare's struggles throughout the remainder of her life.

The tumult resulted in the inevitable conclusion that Francis's growing Order needed an upgrade in its governing apparatus, which meant a more encompassing governing document—a new Rule. The one in use at the time was the Primitive Rule that Francis had cobbled together in 1209 and had been approved by Pope Innocent III. By 1220, however, the Order numbered more than five thousand friars and needed a more cogent document with broader parameters and clearer definitions—and one less dependent on Francis's personal authority.

To this end a general chapter convened in May 1220 shortly after Francis's return, during which they initiated critical decisions. First, it was clear to all, including Francis, that the movement had outgrown the founder's ability to manage it. To help maintain stability under staggering growth, Francis enjoined his friend the bishop of Ostia—Ugolino—to become their official protector and guardian of the order, the leader to shepherd it through this tenuous time. This put Clare in a tough position since, with the recently fashioned *Form of Life*, Ugolino had become her primary antagonist in her resolve to uphold highest poverty.

Ugolino understood that it served everyone's interest to help Francis and his unwieldy order succeed. It was a popular movement, albeit a disordered one. As guardian, Ugolino was poised to harness the religious fervor Francis had tapped and use it to advance the cause of the Church. For this to happen, however, concessions would have to be made, and Francis did not easily abide concessions. To expedite the organization, Ugolino suggested that Francis appropriate an existing Rule to govern the order, just as he would implement for Clare. Francis refused: "I do not want you to mention to me any Rule, whether of Saint Augustine or Saint Bernard or Saint Benedict," he said. "The Lord told me what he wanted:

He wanted me to be a new fool in the world. God did not wish to lead us by any way other than this."[107]

Ugolino "was shocked" and spoke no more of it.[108] And Francis thus set to work fashioning a new and necessary Rule, struggling to keep the terms of his Order true to his original intent. The battle inevitably spilled over into Clare's domain.

---

107 *The Assisi Compilation: FA:ED*, vol. 2, 132–33. This is a thirteenth-century document comprised of anecdotal recollections of early followers of Francis self-described as "we who were with him." It was compiled between 1244 and 1260 as a result of the summons of minister general (in 1244) Cresentius of Iesi to collect as much material as possible about the life of Francis. The collection reflects at times contradictory accounts and tracks, if inadvertently, the ongoing fracturing within the order after Francis's death.

108 *The Assisi Compilation: FA:ED*, vol. 2, 132–33.

CHAPTER 5

|||||||||||||||||||||||||||||||||||||||||||

GRIEF

God, I have told you of my life;
you have placed all my tears in your sight.
All my enemies were plotting evil against me;
they took counsel together.
They repaid me evil for good
and hatred for my love. . .
My friends and my neighbors have drawn near
and have stood against me;
those who were close to me have stayed far away.
You have driven my acquaintances far from me;
they have made me an abomination to them.[109]

his is an excerpt of one of Francis's prayers taken from the psalms, during the latter days of his life.

In the previous chapter I alluded to the years following Francis's return from the Middle East as the beginning of the end for him. These final years of his life similarly track both the summit and the nadir of Clare's life as his truest companion and devoted Lady of the Castle.

Beyond the trouble that awaited him upon his return, Francis was becoming increasingly debilitated by sickness. He had contracted multiple maladies during the year he languished as a prisoner of war

---

109 "The Undated Writings," "At Compline / Antiphon: Holy Virgin Mary / Psalm," *Writings of Saint Francis*, in *FA:ED*, vol. I, 140. The reading is excerpted.

years earlier. In prison he had succumbed to malaria and tuberculosis, the latter of which penetrated his bones. On top of that, while in the desert of Egypt he contracted a malady of the eyes which at first seemed a minor irritation but which quickly became a blinding, festering, and excruciating handicap that left him helpless and in constant pain.

Returning from the east in 1220 and, facing the chaos and discord, he resigned as leader (Minister General) of his own Order. His declining health made it impossible for him to meet the demands of daily oversight. He even considered retreating to a hermitage to live out his days, and to that end, sought counsel from only two trusted sources, one of his brothers—Brother Silvestro—and Clare. She urged him against it and he accepted her counsel.[110] That Francis would turn to Clare for advice at so critical a point in his life reflects the intimate and trusted nature of their bond.

Yet at no time did his reliance upon Clare and her consolation show itself more overtly than it did during these last hard years of Francis's life. What was the nature of their bond, the flower of which bloomed in these last months of his life?

As a friar I spoke with put it, Clare was the one on whom the fatigue of Francis's soul found rest. I add to that: and on Francis's bosom Clare's heartache found peace. Both images capture the intimacy and trust they shared—intimacy of a kind that is rarely realized even in marriage. Many scholars with whom I consulted insist that neither Francis nor Clare was sentimental about their relationship. I've argued[111] that, while some assert it is a stretch of credulity to suggest Francis and Clare loved one another in a romantic way, it is more of a stretch to argue they did not. The standard response says that, while Francis and Clare were very close, their bond took on the form of the love between a father and daughter. Yet all indications suggest otherwise.

Francis had been, after all, Assisi's lead playboy. He was widely remembered as a young stallion roaming the streets at night, leading the

110 *LegMaj*, 12; *FA:ED*, vol. 2, 623.
111 See *Mended*, 41.

pack of Assisi's wild youth in parties and song. His friends had crowned him *dominus*—king—of the party. He had been loved by countless women and he loved them back. He fought his sexual appetite his entire life, even after his conversion. Francis's profligate early life was well known by those closest to him—and by just about everybody else in Assisi. Francis never recoiled from recalling those years of folly. Even after his prolonged conversion, he fought inside himself the continual battle of the temptation of the flesh. When his life was nearing its end and rumors of canonization were afoot, he told his brothers: "Don't canonize me too quickly. I am perfectly capable of fathering a child."[112]

Clare had been the highly desired town beauty pursued by many suitors and no doubt desired by many more. That Francis and Clare would meet and *not* fall in love is far more implausible than the notion that they did fall in love, as young, healthy, sexually formative human beings are wont to do. That they met and found human love and, over time, together agreed to renounce it lends the most plausible explanation for the way their lives unfolded. It accounts for the fact that even before Francis had any thoughts of starting a religious Order, he was building a house for women at San Damiano. It similarly accounts for the meticulous details and planning they

---

112 The citation comes from *Legend of Perugia*, in *St. Francis of Assisi Writings and Early Biographies, English Omnibus of the Sources for the Life of St. Francis* (hereafter cited as *Omnibus*), ed. Marion A. Habig; trans. Raphael Brown, Benen Fahy, Placid Hermann, Paul Oligny, Nest de Robeck, Leo Sherley-Price (Quincy, IL: Franciscan Press, 1991), 1080. It is also found in Bonaventure's *Major Life*, VI:3. The particular translation noted above comes from Julien Green, *God's Fool*, trans. Peter Heinegg (San Francisco: Harper & Row, 1985), 194.

Source material for the early documents relating to Saint Francis is replete with textual difficulties. The early biography known as the *Legend of Perugia* is thought to be compilation of remembrances from the pen of Francis's close friend and amanuensis Brother Leo. A fourteenth-century friar, Ubertino da Casale, notes in a document dated 1305 that certain scrolls (*rotuli*) known to have come from the hand of Brother Leo had been lost. Later he refers again to Brother Leo's scrolls, which he claimed to have had before him, suggesting they had been found. The textual history of the document referred to as the *Legend of Perugia* is beyond the purview of this examination. The writer attributes passages cited from the *Legend of Perugia* as having come from the pen of Brother Leo. All references from this source are found in the *Omnibus*.

undertook in arranging her departure from her family so they could share the same destiny.

There existed a galvanizing energy between them that animated them but that could not be answered by the rules of society, given the disparity in class and rank. And, both being drawn jointly to God, this energy was channeled in a way that enabled them to live together but under the revolutionary vows of poverty, chastity, and obedience. Elsewhere in the sources it says that "from the time that he had been converted to Christ and renounced the world, he had not looked at the face of any woman, except his mother and Saint Clare."[113]

Yet they were not sentimental. They forged a new way—a new religious Order, for both men and women, that carried its own terms and with great care created a symbiosis between the men and the women, binding them to one another in mutual commitment, devotion, courtly grace, and (I dare say) love. It is a beautiful picture and one they fought many battles to protect and defend.

In matters of the human heart, there is no ideal that does not, over time, get slain by real life. And in real life, the high and noble road Clare chose was wrought with detours, stumbling blocks, and no little sorrow. Clare struggled. Her distress, particularly early on, is evidenced in an episode described in a collection of stories about Francis called the *Fioretti* (*Little Flowers*).[114] The episode describes the

113 *2 C*, 112; see *FA:ED*, vol. 2, 322.
114 The *Fioretti*, or "Little Flowers," was originally published in Latin under the title *Actus-Fioretti*. The author did not know Francis's earliest companions, but his good friend, a brother named James of Massa, did. James of Massa had been close to Francis's brothers Masseo, Juniper, Giles, Simon, and Leo, and also to Clare. After the decree of 1266, in which all early legends of Francis had been ordered destroyed, a follow-up summons went out in 1276 soliciting additional material to supplement Bonaventure's biography. Then, it is assumed, that author began scribbling stories about Francis he had heard from James of Massa, who had heard them from the mouths of those "who knew him."

The *Fioretti* is controversial because it arose during a time when the order was splintering into divisions that still exist today, and some assert it is slanted in defense of one position. The strength of the book, however, is the other side of the same coin: the time of its writing. As noted, it was written after the decree of 1266 and was not therefore officially commissioned by a pope or officer of the Church. It is considered an independent source compiled by a sympathetic and diligent writer who *(cont.)*

early years of Clare's religious life when, feeling lonely and isolated, she made a request to share a meal with Francis. She asked him "several times to give her that consolation." But "Francis always refused to grant her that favor." His companions finally prevailed upon him on Clare's behalf, urging him to allow her to come and share a meal. "'Since it seems this way to you, it also seems that way to me,' he [Francis] responded. 'She has been enclosed for a long time in San Damiano and it will do her good to see the place of Saint Mary [the Porziuncola], where she was tonsured and became the spouse of Jesus Christ; and there we will eat together in the name of God.'"[115] When Clare finally went to see him that evening for the dinner, she lingered so long at the Porziuncola that the other sisters at San Damiano grew alarmed, fearing that Francis had sent her to direct another monastery.

Other passages lend additional insight into the nature of their bond. A little-known document written by the provincial minister of Tuscany, known as Brother Thomas of Pavia, recounts words spoken to him directly by Brother Stefano, who lived with Francis in the early days of the Order. (This was the same Brother Stefano who tracked Francis down in Egypt and Syria during his trip to the Middle East.) Thomas wrote that Brother Stefano was "a man of such simplicity and purity of heart that one could hardly imagine his saying anything untrue." Of the many tales Stefano told Thomas about Francis, one that stands out is this: "Brother Stefano also used to say that Blessed Francis did not want to be

---

understood the value of the great stories told by old friends like Leo. Ugolino's work introduces heretofore unpublished and unknown episodes about Francis. The book's weakness is its overblown and phantasmal interpretation of some events, as will be seen, which tends to undermine its believability. In any case, a careful and discriminating examination of it renders the astute reader nuggets of authenticity and simplicity about Francis and his friends that ring true. The epigraph reads: "This book contains certain little flowers, miracles, and inspiring stories of the glorious little poor man of Christ, Saint Francis, and some of his holy companions as revealed by their successors which were omitted in his biographies but which are also very useful and edifying."

115 *Fioretti, FA:ED,* vol. 3, 590. As for his hesitancy to have her come to the Porziuncola, one can only speculate. Women were forbidden there, generally, so he and his brothers broke protocol by allowing her to come. Beyond that, it is conceivable that he wanted to avoid possible temptations of a carnal nature.

on familiar terms with any woman and he did not permit any woman to become familiar with him; only with the blessed Clare did he seem to show affection."[116] Eventually, as the official record of Francis's life was rewritten for the purposes of canonization and the consolidation of the Order, Clare's role in his personal life became greatly diminished.

But getting back to the time when Francis stepped down as Minister General, Francis set to work on rewriting the Rule for the growing Order. This ended up being an ordeal for him for a variety of reasons that are too convoluted to discuss here.[117] Suffice it to say, the final Rule was a far cry from his intended revision and only alienated him further from his Order.

In stepping down, Francis had thought he secured oversight of the Order by transferring its leadership to a trusted friend, Peter of Catani (one of his first followers). But in 1221 Peter died unexpectedly. At that point, Francis lost all control. Worse, he even lost influence over the direction the Order would take. For those who clamored for a new, more "reasonable" Rule, Francis had become a problem. He was becoming increasingly isolated and, more shockingly, some of the newer brothers were heaping ridicule and abuse upon him. He was left in exile, unceremoniously dismissed and alienated from his own Order. Francis knew he had to leave the Porziuncola. And the decisions he made in accordance with this necessity would define his legacy. The first decision he made was to retreat to a mountain hermitage in Tuscany called La Verna. The second (in due course) was to return to San Damiano.

La Verna

It is impossible to know Francis without confronting what happened to him at La Verna.

---

116 *Miscellaneous Franciscan Sources, FA:ED*, vol. 3, 794.
117 For a detailed account of this arduous and excruciating *process* for Francis, see *Mended*, 123.

La Verna was a remote hermitage in Tuscany, owned by a wealthy landed knight named Count Orlando dei Chiusi. In the early years (around the time Clare joined Francis), the count had heard Francis preach and was inspired to offer him his mountain as a place of retreat, calling it "very solitary and wild." It stood high on a steep precipice shrouded in tall pines and riddled with jutting crags. The landscape was extreme—the kind that reached into the deepest corners of Francis's soul, as he was viscerally connected to the heartbeat of the land.

He went there with a few of his closest companions at a time when his Order had, for all practical purposes, rejected him, and when the illnesses from his youth were gaining ground over his physical well-being. He was in constant pain from dyspepsia and the more recently contracted burning of his eyes.

What happened one night when he was awake, perhaps tormented by the devil in his pain (as he often felt was the case),[118] remains a mystery, and one which the brother present with him at the time, Brother Leo, spoke very little about thereafter. Leo had left Francis alone at night, at Francis's request, so that he could pray. And the next time Leo saw Francis in the early hours before dawn the next morning, Francis had incurred wounds. These were not typical wounds such as might have occurred if he had tripped on a root or turned an ankle. The wounds Leo saw were symmetrically placed, one on each hand, one on each foot, and one on the side of his chest. These wounds, of course, mimicked the very wounds Jesus Christ suffered when he was executed by crucifixion. Francis's wounds were atypical in another way. Images in the art of the time represent them as bloody impressions that, with proper medical care, might have been stitched. Francis's actual wounds, however, were not impressions. They were "three-dimensional," as one friar described it to me, meaning they jutted out, as if his hands and feet bore actual nails.

---

118 He would call to Brother Leo: "'The devils, brother, have beaten me severely. I wish you would keep me company because I am afraid to be alone,'" Leo recounts. "Every bone in Francis's body was trembling." Leo "remained close to him all night." *AC: FA:ED*, vol. 2, 225.

In the Catholic tradition, when a person of holiness bears the marks of Christ's crucifixion, the miracle is called receiving the stigmata. It is deemed the most precious of all miraculous gifts, setting apart the holy person as uniquely and perfectly representing the life of Jesus. Few saints can claim the gift,[119] and it is always difficult to verify. In Francis's case, once Leo discovered him in such a state, Francis went to great lengths to conceal the wounds, something that would have been a challenge. Henceforth he could barely walk and would have had difficulty even feeding himself. He would have been in excruciating and constant pain, as you or I would be if we had five fixed nails protruding from our flesh at various points on the body.

When I examined this episode in my biography of Francis, I mentioned that I had consulted two physicians about whether a person's psychological frame of mind could create such a dramatic physical result, and both conceded that the human body can mimic, in physical symptoms, the state of mind that may be consuming the thoughts and longings of a person. They both independently cited the phenomenon of false pregnancy, called pseudocyesis.[120] From the earliest days of his religious awakening, Francis was a literalist—he took his religious impulses as actual marching orders, not abstract principles to ponder and pontificate about. When he had the vision beneath the cross in the ruins of San Damiano, hearing God tell him, "Rebuild my church," Francis did not write a tome and post a thesis about how to reform a corrupted institution. He picked up stones and started measuring. When he renounced his family and his place in Assisi's merchant class, he did not quietly put away his French linens and slip a note under the door of the family home. He stood in the public square, stripped off his linens to the point of nakedness, and placed the linens in a bundle into the hands of his thunderstruck father, publicly and forever severing himself from his

---

119 A few of the saints in Catholicism who are said to have received the stigmata include Saint Padre Pio of Pietrelcina, Saint Rita of Cascia, and the Apostle Paul (see Galatians 6:17), among others.

120 *Mended*, 140.

family and renouncing his family name. Most significantly, when Francis learned the words of the Lord wherein Jesus explained what it meant to be a follower—"If you want to be perfect, go, sell your possessions and give to the poor, and you will have treasure in heaven; then come, follow me" (Matt. 19:21)—he appropriated these commands right down to the tunic. Francis did not live in abstractions, and so any identification with Christ's sufferings that he might have pondered similarly would not have been abstract. They would have been actual. Christ bore five wounds; Francis incurred five wounds.

The Catholic Church deems the stigmata the highest and most privileged miracle, and the testimony in the investigation related to Francis's canonization affirms the presence of these wounds. The official version of what happened on Mount La Verna is recounted this way by two early biographers: "His hands and feet seemed to be pierced through the middle by nails, with the heads of the nails appearing on the inner part of his hands and on the upper part of his feet, and their points protruding on opposite sides,"[121] writes Thomas of Celano. Another biographer, Henri d'Avranches, adds: Francis "saw in a vision a six-winged seraph, as it were, fastened to a cross with its arms stretched out and feet bound together. And though for a long time he pondered with anxious spirit what this strange sort of vision might portend, he understood nothing about it clearly. Lo, and behold, the prints of nails, as it were, appeared in his hands and feet and his right side was pierced as though by a lance. The palms of his hands and the tops of his feet were swollen."[122]

---

121 *1C, FA:ED,* vol. I, 264.
    Henri d'Avranches writes, in d'Avranches, *VL, FA:ED,* vol. I, 510:
        So does Jesus' passion remain implanted in his heart,
        So imprinted right through the marrow of his soul
        That it cannot be hid, but must flood outwardly
        And mark its likeness on his partnered flesh,
        Becoming visible, as it were, through transparent limbs.
        The five wounds of the Redeemer appear impressed
        In their separate places.
122 *LJS, FA:ED,* vol. I, 410.

For his part, Leo—though he was present with Francis when the wounds appeared—only once mentioned them in his writings. In all the works attributed to him—and none more than Leo went to great lengths to preserve Francis's memory—the only remark he made about the wounds was this: "The vision of the seraph filled his soul with consolation and united him closely to God for the remainder of his life."[123]

When I taught a college course on Saint Francis years ago in Italy, one of my students remarked almost matter-of-factly, "I think Francis did it to himself." Pondering it, I could not deny that possibility—if that was indeed the case, it would have been completely consistent with the way Francis lived.

I am not here to confirm or debunk the miraculous nature of the presence of the stigmata on Francis's body at the end of his life. I simply recognize that such marks render a consistent culmination of the life he lived and the sensibilities he maintained throughout his life. In whatever way these wounds were incurred, it makes perfect sense, as his life drew to its painful close, that his body would bear the marks of the cross of Christ. The point is, in the late fall of 1224, in the midst of great sorrow and physical struggle, during a retreat on the Mount La Verna, Francis incurred debilitating wounds that mimicked the wounds of Christ.

He left the mountain a few months later riding on a mule while Leo walked beside him. Together they made the long journey back home to Francis's beloved Assisi, where he again attempted to find rest at the Porziuncola. But alas, as Leo wrote, "We who were with him witnessed often with our own eyes frequently how some of the brothers did not provide for his needs or said something that would offend."[124] As he faced fears and sadness, failings and losses, on top of deteriorating health, Francis needed rest. And so he made the decision to go to the only place where he could find it. He went to Clare.[125]

---

123 *Legend of Perugia*, in *Omnibus*, vol. II, 1070.
124 *Legend of Perugia*, in *Omnibus*, vol. II, 1082.
125 Of the legends and other writings, only two mention this period in its entirety, and both sources are attributed to Leo (*Legend of Perugia*, the *Mirror of Perfection*; (contd.)

Return to San Damiano

Francis, by this point, had been so debilitated, reduced to dependency upon others, blind and in constant pain, he found that the only place he could hope to gain rest was back where it all began for him, under the attendance of the one for whom his entire enterprise had been initiated—San Damiano and Clare. This short season brought to full flower the bond they shared and had forged over many years of trial and struggle. While his sufferings distressed Clare, as sufferings would for any loved one, the weeks he rested (or attempted to) at San Damiano would have been for Clare the culmination of love and devotion befitting the Lady and her Knight.

Early 1225 would begin the last full year of Francis's life. That is when he returned to San Damiano, where Clare established for him a small hut for privacy and repose. Though Francis fiercely hid his five wounds from all others, he freely exposed them to Clare and she took measurements. She intended to make him shoes that accommodated the wounds' protrusions.[126]

The straw hut, alas, proved attractive to field mice, and they tormented Francis relentlessly, day and night. He found little rest there.

Even so, amid his suffering, a picture of clarity arose in him during his short season at San Damiano, and he felt the need to write a song. "I wish to compose a new 'praises of the Lord' for his creatures," he said, because "these creatures minister to our needs every day. Without them we could not live."[127] The song has been called "The Canticle of the Creatures," and it summoned all elements of the natural world to render to God the thanks due him.[128] "All praise be Yours, my Lord, through all You have made, and

---

the episode is also mentioned in the *Fioretti*.) Some biographers do not mention Francis's stay at San Damiano at all (Bonaventure and Henri d'Avranches); and Thomas of Celano, in his *Second Life*, acknowledges only that when Francis "was more worn out than usual because of various serious discomforts from his illnesses . . . it was at then that he composed the *Praise of the Creatures*." (2C, *FA:ED* vol. 2, 384 and 385; emphasis in original. Even so, no mention is made that the "Praise of the Creatures"—the Canticle, as it is known—was written at San Damiano.)

126 These shoes are on display in the Relic Room at the Basilica of San Francesco in Assisi.

127 *Legend of Perugia*, in *Omnibus*, vol. II, 1021.

128 Francis composed it in Umbrian (not Latin) because he had the common (contd.)

first [from] Brother Sun, who illumines God's presence and is the *porta significatione*—doorway to meaning. He is warm and grand, and radiates the life force of God."[129] The Canticle continues, "All praise be Yours, my Lord, through Sister Moon because she is precious and beautiful and clear"—*clarite*, Clare's name—"the light bearer and reflector of the sun's brilliance. . . . All praise . . . through Sister Earth, who, through gentle assertions, governs all life on the planet, bringing forth fruit and colorful flowers and herbs. All praise to God through Brother Wind, who spreads seed and moves waters, and who is sometimes serene and sometimes fierce. All praise to God through Sister Water, who nourishes the earth through a force that is unstoppable, cleansing, chaste, and healing. All praise to God when peace reigns between neighbors, for to live in peace requires meekness and charity—the mark of humility and true humanity. Even Sister Death renders praise to God, for no person can escape it. They are blessed who face mortality in God's 'most holy will.' "[130]

In this song, Francis calls all members of creation to give back to God the gifts he ascribed to them. All creatures have been fashioned to participate in a cosmic performance sung in every landscape for the singular purpose of rendering back to God the beauty and originality of his personality. For Francis, the Canticle reflects the vision of God that brings all that exists in this world into harmony in unified praise

---

people in mind. He wanted them to be able to sing it, for he intended it to be sung. He sang it himself. Interestingly, in it, there is no mention made of animals.

129 Francis says of the sun, quoted in the *Legend of Perugia:* "The sun is the most beautiful of all creatures because it is the one which, better than all the others, could be compared to God. At sunrise every person ought to praise God for having created this heavenly body which gives light to our eyes during the day; at evening, when night falls, everyone ought to praise God for that other creature, our brother fire, which enables our eyes to see clearly in the darkness. We are all like blind people, and through these two creatures God gives us light. Therefore, for these two creatures and for the others that serve us each day, we ought to praise their glorious Creator in a very special way." *Legend of Perugia*, in *Omnibus*, vol. II, 1022.

130 This is explored in detail in *Mended*, ch. 12, 133ff.

of its Creator.[131] To write it, Francis had to place himself where he could hear it—at peace and at rest, with Clare. Then creation raised its voice and Francis heard it and, in a small way, Eden was restored during this last brief visitation between them. Clare and Francis found it together—perfect love, joining all creation in the upward reach of earth to heaven.

And here marks the last time Francis and Clare would see one another on this earth. After several months, the time had come for Francis to depart. He had been strongly urged by Bishop Ugolino to have special treatment for his eyes, and the bishop made the necessary arrangements. Francis was bound for a town called Rieti, where he would undergo a barbaric treatment for his eyes. So, in July 1225, at the behest of his friends, Francis "consoled [Clare] with holy and honey-sweet words and said good-bye to her humbly, as he usually did."[132]

Sister Death

There is no point in rehearsing the excruciating episodes that would mark the last year of Francis's life, between the fall of 1225 and the fall of 1226. The eye treatment availed him nothing save more pain. Inasmuch as one human body can endure the maximum measure of pain without succumbing, Francis suffered it. The last months of his life were marked by a level of suffering that could be likened to the physical suffering of his beloved Lord.

The level of heartache Clare was experiencing through it all can only be speculated about. At all points during Francis's final months, she was sure she would see him again and was waiting for that day. Even so, she began experiencing symptoms of a physical malady that left her

---

131 The song is sometimes glossed over as sentimental or reduced to the misguided notion that in it Francis "worshiped" nature. In the Canticle Francis summons creation to give back to God the beauty and originality he bestowed on them. Creation is the agent. God is the recipient. It is not pantheism. It is an exercise in the particulars—sun, moon, wind, fire, points of intersection between this world and the next. God is ever the giver.

132 *Fioretti*, in *Omnibus*, vol. II, 1344. Armstrong's version reads "holy words," *FA:ED*, vol. III, 599.

immobile. But at the point at which Clare became painfully aware that Francis's physical deterioration would lead to his death, in late September 1226, she was overwhelmed with the thought that she would not see him again. In fact, she was so ill and so incapacitated that she thought *she* might actually precede *him* in death. She sent word, through a brother, of her sorrow at the thought of not seeing him again and it broke his heart to hear it. He sent back a word of consolation: "Tell her to banish the sorrow and sadness she feels at the thought of never seeing me again. Tell her that before she dies she will see me again and will receive great consolation from me."[133]

It is not known if Francis thought he would rally strength enough to visit her one more time. If that is what he thought, he was wrong. He did not rally. He left his earthly tent in the early hours of October 3, 1226. He had requested of his brothers, "When you see me *in extremis* lay me down naked on the earth and leave me there for as long as it takes to walk a leisurely mile." And, as requested, when the throes of death descended, they laid him naked on the ground, while his closest companions surrounded him, giving voice to the song of praise he wrote, the Canticle. He whispered to a brother, "I have done what is mine to do. May Christ teach you what is yours to do." Then he uttered his final words, "I call upon you, O Lord. Come quickly to me."

The brothers stayed true to the promise Francis made to Clare that she would see him again. They prepared his body for temporary burial in San Giorgio, a small church inside the walls of Assisi, and they made the trek up the hill toward town, bringing him first to San Damiano for Clare's final look.

Of the writers who attempted to capture the scene, Francis's first biographer, Thomas of Celano, paints a poignant picture. The words rendered here suggest that the sentiment reflected that of all the Poor Sisters at San Damiano. There is a degree to which this could be true in theory. Yet it must be remembered that it was Clare alone whom Francis

133 *Legend of Perugia*, in *Omnibus*, vol. II, 1085.

comforted with honey-sweet words, Clare alone whose care he tended to; it was only Clare's face he knew. So the words captured by Thomas, at their core, singularly capture Clare's lament:

> The Lady Clare! . . .
> They looked upon him,
> groaning and weeping with great anguish of heart.
> "Father, O father, what shall we do? . . . Why are you abandoning us poor women? We are forsaken! To whom are you entrusting us? Why didn't you send us ahead of you in joy to the place you are going, instead of leaving us behind in sorrow? What would you have us do, enclosed in this cell, without your usual visits? All consolation ebbs away along with you, just as no solace remains for us who are buried to the world! Who will comfort us in so great a poverty? . . . Who will help us in temptation? You, who experienced so many temptations! You, who were such a careful judge of temptations! Who will comfort us in the midst of distress? You, who were so often our help in times of distress! What bitter separation, what painful absence!"[134]

The writer who, in my mind, captured the clearest picture of Clare's grief was Jacopone da Todi, who wrote in verse of Clare's seeing Francis's body and clutching his hand:

> . . . Saint Clare came,
> bringing her sisters with her;
> greedy for such treasure she tried in vain
> to pull out those nails with her teeth.[135]

134 *1 C*, X, 117; *CA:ED*, 402.
135 Laud 61: "O Francesco Povero." *FA:ED*, vol. 3, 874.

||||||||||||||||||||||||||||||||||||||||||||

Part
Two

||||||||||||||||||||||||||||||||||||||||||||

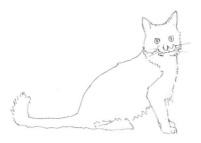

CHAPTER 6

IIIIIIIIIIIIIIIIIIIIIIIIIIIIIIIIIIIIIIIIIIIII

BATTLE LINES

The thought that comes to mind at this point in Clare's story is "drop curtain." Intermission. Everybody take a breath and wait for a bit while the cast regroups, finds its second wind, and reclaims the stage.

The period immediately following Francis's death goes dark when it comes to Clare's activities. One telling detail does emerge: her mother, Ortolana, took up residency at San Damiano that year, 1226, the year Francis died. If Ortolana took religious vows at the time, it is not noted in the record. Perhaps she simply came to Clare, as any loving mother would, at a time of grief and personal crisis. Regardless, Ortolana is said to have come to the "same Order as her holy daughter, blessed Clare, and lived in it with the other sisters in great humility. There, adorned by religious and holy deeds, she passed from this life."[136]

Two forces were pressing on Clare at this time that would set her trajectory and establish new terms of this changing picture. The first would be the ascent of Ugolino to the papacy in 1227, and the other was Clare's continued debilitation from a lingering illness. We'll explore them in turn, with the latter first.

---

136 *PC* 1,5; *CA:ED* 146: This is the testimony of Sister Pacifica de Guelfuccio of Assisi, the First Witness. Ortolana seems to have died there prior to 1238 since her name does not appear on the list of sisters whose names are found on a document published by Luke Wadding concerning the sale of property, see *Annales Minorum*, vol. III, 14-15.

Clare's Illness

Angela Seracchioli said that "when Francis died, that was the end of her, physically speaking. She never left her bed." Clare would leave her bed on occasion thereafter; however, never again would she do so without the assistance of her sisters. Clare's life from this point on is no longer measured in linear movements such as could be traced from her childhood in the neighborhood of San Rufino, to her secret meetings with Francis, to her flight from the family home, to her brief stints at San Paolo and Sant'Angelo, till finally landing sure-footed at her permanent dwelling place at San Damiano. Her intention, even then, had been to engage actively with the surrounding community as the Franciscan brothers did. At one point she even expressed the desire to travel to Morocco to die for Christ, in the wake of four friars having been martyred there.[137]

This and all other dreams died the day in early October when Francis shed his earthly tent, leaving Clare to find her own way amid rising external pressures. Things were going very wrong for Clare. Nothing was playing out according to the intended script. How could Francis abandon her? How could she lose her mobility? She was supposed to have been his partner in service; she was supposed to have been able to stand on her own two feet.

New terms were being drawn. Her life's mission and her spiritual vision, from now on, would be executed and exercised from the confines of her bed. Apart from a few external historical contingencies that intruded upon her life in San Damiano, which forced her to rise from her bed and act in response, her world now was otherwise traceable by the world she inhabited inside her mind.

---

137 All references from *Process* in this section are taken from *CA:ED*, 139-196. From *PC* 6,6: "She also said Lady Clare had such a fervent spirit she willingly wanted to endure martyrdom for love of the Lord. She showed this when, after she had heard certain brothers had been martyred in Morocco, she said she wanted to go there. Then, because of this, the witnesses wept. This was before she was so sick. Asked who was present at this, she replied that those who were present had died." [Sixth Witness, Sister Cecilia, daughter of Sir Gualtieri Cacciaguerra of Spoleto]

Details and specifics related to what actually afflicted Clare physically are absent from the record. We are helped a little by some of the testimonies in the *Process of Canonization* that made passing references to her illness. The first witness said, "[W]hen she was so sick that she could not get up from bed, she had herself raised to sit up and be supported with some cushions behind her back. She spun [thread], so from her work she made corporals and altar linens for almost all the churches of the plains and hills around Assisi."[138] The same witness added later in her testimony, "While she was healthy, she served [the sick] and washed their feet and gave them water with her own hands."[139] Another witness noted, "Blessed Clare, before she was sick, practiced great abstinence."[140] And then another: "After she had heard certain brothers had been martyred in Morocco, she said she wanted to go there. . . . This was before she was so sick."[141]

The exact nature of her illness is unknown, and opinions vary. Loek Bosch, a Franciscan friar who lived at San Damiano several years ago, told me that some thought Clare had multiple sclerosis. Another scholar I spoke with thought she might have had rheumatic fever.[142] Many dismissed her malady as a result of her strict fasting, and Sister Anastasia Chiara, a nun currently living in the convent of the Poor Clares in Assisi, said that some regarded it as a sort of "mystical illness."[143]

One historian I interviewed suggested a possibility that seemed most plausible: that Clare may have contracted tuberculosis, which entered her bone. Tuberculosis spread rampantly across Europe in the Middle

---

138 *PC*, 1, 11, Sister Pacifica de Guelfuccio, first witness.
139 *PC* 1,12. Also: 1, 17, 67. Asked about the time Saint Clare began that long illness, she replied she believed it was twenty-nine years. Note: While Sister Pacifica claims that St. Clare was sick for twenty-nine years, the Legend 39 maintains twenty-eight years. For a thorough treatment of the illness of Saint Clare, see Oktavian Schumucki, "Infermità," *Dizionario Francescano* (Padova, IT: Edizioni Messagero Padova, 1983): 725–70.
140 *PC* 2, second witness.
141 *PC* 6, sixth witness.
142 Chiara Frugoni in a personal interview by e-mail, June 2007.
143 This discussion occurred in a face-to-face conversation that took place in November 2006.

Ages and became its primary epidemic, overtaking leprosy as the more aggressive, faster-killing disease. Tuberculosis of the bone is rare, but it can be manifested in someone whose body carries the germ, especially if the body's resistance has been broken down. It is worth noting that Francis himself contracted tuberculosis (TB) during his year of imprisonment in Perugia, in his early twenties. He would have still been carrying it during the years of his religious conversion and his developing friendship with Clare. Given the proximate nature of their bond, it is possible that Clare could have contracted it from Francis, with her symptoms emerging later, as her resistance was worn down through fasting and other abstinences. TB enters the bones and joints by way of the bloodstream and attacks primarily the spine and long-bone extremities. A person with bone TB suffers pain, swelling, stiffness, muscle weakness—that is, true weakness (or "objective weakness" because of damaged motor neurons)—and decreased appetite or anorexia—symptoms Clare similarly exhibited. Unless it is treated quickly, it can result in deformity or crippling.

Nevertheless, the fact remains that without pathology testing, the specific nature of Clare's malady cannot be known.[144]

Francis knew before his death that Clare was ailing and would need extra physical care. When he was staying at San Damiano near the end of his life and wrote the "Canticle of the Creatures," he also composed another canticle for Clare and her sisters. In it, he gently exhorts the sisters to bear patiently the burden of caring for one another's physical ailments. He wrote, "Those who are weighed down by sickness, and the others who are wearied because of them, all of you: bear it in peace. For you will sell this fatigue at a very high price."[145] In the same canticle, Francis also touched

144 Her symptoms are consistent with bone tuberculosis as described in Edwin S. Wilson Jr. and Edward G. Whiting Jr., "Disseminated Tuberculosis of Bone," *California Medicine* 105, no. 4 (1966): 284–287.

145 Leo writes about the circumstances of the composition of this Canticle in the *Legend of Perugia*, in *Omnibus*, vol. II, 1024–1025: "When he thought of [the sisters] his spirit was always moved to pity because he knew that from the beginning of their conversion they had led and were still leading an austere and poor life by free choice and out of necessity. He especially asked them to treat their bodies with discernment and discretion, and to use alms God would send them with joy and (contd.)

upon another point of contention that he knew would affect Clare and how she would live out her days: "Do not look at the life outside, for that of the Spirit is better."[146] Whether Francis was suggesting here that Clare would be well-served to embrace enclosure (the cloister) and abandon all hope of a mendicant existence is irrelevant. Clare had lost the ability to walk; this alone left her no choice but to accept the inevitable change that was overtaking the female monasteries of the Franciscans under the rule of Ugolino, now Pope Gregory IX: the sisters in convents all over Europe were destined to be cloistered.

The only issue not yet resolved for Clare was the nature of their poverty. Would they maintain the mandate as Francis outlined it for his brothers and for the sisters—depending upon the aid of the brothers, alms, and community service to sustain their lives? Or would they rest securely on property secured with dowries with no worries about paying the rent?

Pope Gregory IX: Poor Sisters or Enclosed Nuns?

That question encapsulates the other critical force that was pressing in on Clare, a force that would summon her from a grief-stricken stupor and animate her purpose. That would be the ascent in early 1227 of Bishop Ugolino, the guardian of the Order and her personal friend, to the papacy a few months after Francis's death. He would set in motion a series of objectives that would create nothing short of a tectonic shift in the Franciscan movement and challenge all that Clare and Francis had fought so effectually to preserve—that is, her unstinting resolve to uphold Francis's particular version of what it meant to assume the "privilege of poverty."

Apart from the changes that were percolating among Francis's (male) Order, Pope Gregory IX undertook a vigorous campaign to organize the

---

thanksgiving. He recommended that the healthy sisters bear patiently with the fatigue brought on by their care of the sick, and that the latter endure their sicknesses and their needs with patience."

146 "The Canticle of Exhortation to Saint Clare and Her Sisters" (1225); *CA:ED*, 394.

female religious societies under a singular paradigm, imposing on them all the Rule of St. Benedict. This meant these women's societies would own properties and receive dowries, which likewise meant security (wealth), autonomy (no need to depend upon the brothers), and enclosure (no longer engaging with the community). The Italian scholar Chiara Frugoni, in her book *Una solitudine abitata: Chiara d'Assisi,* explores this theme in the story of Clare as it is depicted in Giotto's fresco cycle (fourteenth century) in the Upper Basilica of San Francesco in Assisi.[147] She highlights Giotto's image of a grief-stricken Clare beholding the dead Francis which, according to Frugoni, captures the real story of what was going on at the time and what Clare was up against (see page 196). The church in the background of the image is depicted as opulent and pristine while at the same time is represented as a prison, the cloister. "Francesco is indeed dead and Chiara and the sisters cry against the background of a rich San Damiano, an opulent golden prison of their enclosure."[148] The image, according to Frugoni, represents the new program being imposed by Gregory on female monasteries all over Italy and attempted on the Poor Sisters at San Damiano.

At this time, the evolution of the Franciscan Orders was unfolding both for the men and women. Changes were being made under Gregory's influence that reconfigured the priorities and the way of life of the brothers. Gregory had been instrumental in hammering out the revised Rule that Francis eschewed. Even before Francis died, the undercurrents of change were working over the landscape of his experiment. The ideals he championed, which ignited so bold an enterprise, were being decisively reconfigured so as to be less severe and more manageable. Gregory clearly understood the promise the Franciscan model held forth—he was, after all, the pope who canonized

147 The fresco cycle is based upon the *Major Life,* written in 1260 by then-Minister General Bonaventure as the definitive biography of Saint Francis.

148 Frugoni, *Una solitudine abitata: Chiara d'Assisi,* 52–53 (author's translation from the Italian). She asserts that the image coincides with the effort being undertaken at the time to gradually conceal Clare's place in Francis's story, calling such an effort "progressive concealment."

Francis. But he also saw the lack of sustainability in the real world of institutional governance. As one writer put it, "While Gregory respected the memory of Francis, the saint's radical way of life was not a helpful guide."[149]

Pope Gregory IX envisioned a more academic and ecclesiastical role for the brothers whose numbers, by then, had reached into the tens of thousands. They could not all be beggars. Indeed, their devotion and reforming zeal, conversely, could well serve to advance and undergird the engagement of the laity in the Mother Church. These changes would unfold over the years and decades immediately following Francis's death. But Gregory, who controlled the destiny of both the male and female Franciscan communities in his time, turned the ship into a differing tide.

Any changes of milieu among the brothers meant, of necessity, changes for the sisters, since Francis and Clare had resolved that the two groups would be inextricably bound to one another. As Gregory moved the men toward a more sedentary and academic existence, this left them less able to beg alms in order to care for the women. Try as they might, the care of the quickly multiplying women's monasteries could not be sustained by the friars. This predicament could have been exacerbated in part by Gregory's pushing the women into enclosure, limiting their ability to generate income on their own. Regardless, the life of poverty these women aspired to was unsustainable and ultimately self-defeating. "The poverty experiment had not gone well. Nuns were suffering in monasteries too poor to sustain them, and the Franciscan brothers taking care of these nuns were needed for ecclesiastical service."[150]

Navigating the papal bulls on this point demands more rigor and nuance than this study requires. We'll simply highlight that, at this point of his pontificate, Gregory sympathized with and even adored the Poor

149 Mueller, *Privilege of Poverty*, 34.
150 Mueller, *Privilege of Poverty*, 34.

Sisters and especially Clare. To that end, giving a nod to his sentimental side, in a bull issued in December 1227, he consented, in theory, to the idea of the brothers caring for the sisters, that they "should have care and concern for those committed to your guard as if they were your sheep."[151]

Shortly thereafter Gregory made an unplanned visit to Assisi. It is worth noting the reasons for this, since it involves another key figure who would loom large in Clare's story.

Frederick II

When Ugolino ascended to the papal throne in 1227, among other urgencies, he promptly ordered Frederick II to keep a promise he had made to wage a crusade in the Holy Land. In August 1227, in response to Gregory's command, Frederick attempted to carry out his promised crusade. But he was felled by a fever, which derailed his program, so Gregory's injunction went unheeded. This affronted Gregory and led the pope to excommunicate Frederick in September 1227, terminating what had been a tenuous peace between them.

The relationship between the pope and the "Holy Roman Emperor" had always been fraught with hazards, since the paradigm of this relationship in the early Middle Ages had the emperor ruling alongside the pope. The pope was subject to the emperor politically, while the emperor bowed beneath the spiritual mantle of the pope, who crowned him. For a time, this mutuality manifested itself in secular emperors utilizing holy offices of the Church as tentacles of power which, predictably, eroded the congeniality. At one point, around 1072, Pope Gregory VII issued a decree forbidding church officials to serve in this secular capacity. This prompted Emperor Frederick I—Frederick "Barbarossa," Frederick II's grandfather—to establish a network of dukes in order to maintain local order in their stead. Additionally, he took charge of another arm of power to consolidate his authority, the *ministerialia*—former military men. This new order of armed champions became the defining model of military prowess of the age—noble knighthood. So, by the time of

---

151 See Mueller, *Privilege*, 142, notes 18–20.

Francis (who aspired to such knighthood) and Clare and their contemporary Frederick II, the lines had been drawn between the office of the Church and the political power of the emperor. The two entities existed ever in tension to maintain the edge of power over the other.

After Gregory IX's excommunication of Frederick II, the Emperor fomented revolt against the pope. This culminated in an attack at Saint Peter's Basilica itself during a Mass on Easter Tuesday in 1239, when even some of the pope's guards abandoned him. Thus came to pass the pope's unplanned visit to Assisi.

During this tempestuous time, having fled the mob in Rome for Assisi's "county seat" of Spoleto, all thoughts, plans, and energies of Gregory's centered on advancing "the cult of the saint," meaning Francis, to shore up his base, and he turned his focus to Assisi. His issued the bull *Recolentes*, announcing his intention to build a basilica (*specialis ecclesia*) to house Francis's mortal remains, and a few months later he undertook Francis's canonization. Concomitant to the canonization, he laid the foundation stone of the basilica and commissioned Francis's follower, Thomas of Celano, to write the first official biography.

Gregory was enthusiastically received in Assisi, predictably; more importantly, he paid a visit to Clare. This episode highlighted the profusive nature of his affection for her while demonstrating his tireless effort to work his will over her designs.

What transpired over the course of this visit is documented in the *Legend of Saint Clare*:

> Pope Gregory of happy memory, a man as very worthy of the papal throne as he was venerable in his deeds, loved this holy woman intensely with a fatherly affection. When he was [attempting to] persuade her that, because of the events of the times and the dangers of the world, she should consent to have some possessions which he himself willingly offered, she resisted with a very strong spirit and would in no way acquiesce.

To this the Pope replied: "If you fear for your vow, We absolve you from it." She said, "Holy Father, I will never in any way wish to be absolved from the following of Christ."

She received with great joy the fragments of alms and the scraps of bread that the questors brought and, as if saddened by whole [loaves of] bread, she rejoiced more in the scraps.

What else?

By the most perfect poverty

she was eager to conform to the Poor Crucified,

so that nothing transitory would separate

the lover from her Beloved

or would impede her way with the Lord.

Behold, two miracles took place which this lover of poverty merited to perform.[152]

In the pope's effort to consolidate the female communities under "the Ugolinian model,"[153] he elevated his nephew, Cardinal Rainaldo, to succeed him as the guardian protector of the female societies. Rainaldo quickly established both his position and his mandate in a letter he issued in August 1228 to all of the existing women's societies in Italy, celebrating Gregory's ascendance and announcing his own new role as guardian. The recipients included the monasteries at San Damiano, Santa Maria of Vallegloria, Perugia, Foligno, Florence, Lucca, Siena, Arezzo, Borgo, Acquaviva, Narni, Città di Castello, Todi, Santa Serphia of Cortona, Faenza, Milan, Padua, Trent, Verona, Orvieto, Gubbio, San Paolo of Terni, San Paolo of Spoleto and Cortona.[154] Rainaldo listed San Damiano first as if to emphasize that the pope had successfully brought this seminal and

---

152 *LCl* 14; *CA:ED*, 300.

153 Essentially, the Benedictine model.

154 Mueller, *Privilege*, 39. See also "La fortuna del movimento damianita in Italia (sec. XIII): propositi per un censimento da fare," in *Chiara di Assisi: Atti del XX Convegno internazionale degli Società internazionale di studi francescani e Centro interuniversitaio di studi francescani held in Assisi 15–17 ottobre 1992*, ed. Enrico Menesto (Spoleto: Centro italiano di studi sull'Alto Medioevo, 1993), 73–78.

(by now) widely acclaimed community under his model. The problem was, Clare had not surrendered her domain to it and, beyond that, had petitioned the pope for an exemption from his plan, which Gregory remitted, reluctantly.

A month after Rainaldo's letter, Gregory IX issued a document reiterating Clare's initial request and then confirming it with his apostolic authority:

Gregory, Bishop, Servant of the servants of God, to his beloved daughters in Christ, Clare and the other servants of Christ gathered together in the church of San Damiano of the diocese of Assisi, health and apostolic benediction.

As is evident, you have renounced the desire for all temporal things, desiring to dedicate yourselves to the Lord alone. Because of this, since you have sold all things and given them to the poor, you propose not to have any possessions whatsoever, clinging in all things to the footprints of Him, the Way, the Truth, and the Life Who, for our sake, was made poor. Nor does a lack of possessions frighten you from a proposal of this sort; for the left hand of the heavenly Spouse is under your head to support the weakness of your body, which you have placed under the law of your soul through an ordered charity. Finally, He Who feeds the birds of the heavens and clothes the lilies of the field will not fail you in either food or clothing, until He ministers to you in heaven, when His right hand especially will more happily embrace you in the fullness of His sight. Therefore, we confirm with our apostolic authority, as you requested, your proposal of most high poverty, granting you by the authority of [those] present that no one can compel you to receive possessions.[155]

---

155 "The *Privilege of Poverty* of Pope Gregory IX" (1228), *CA:ED*, 87.

The next time there would be a papal document relating to the Order's situation was in 1247 in a "form of life" issued by Gregory's successor, Pope Innocent IV. In the meantime, Clare contended with Gregory IX, whose intentions for the women's societies were well known and unrelenting. Despite Gregory's concession, he nevertheless deemed it a temporary arrangement that, as time did its work, would give way to the larger agenda he was working out for female Orders. As Joan Mueller describes it, "From Gregory's perspective, Clare's treasured 'privilege of poverty' was a temporary compromise that he hoped Clare and her sisters would outgrow."[156]

Not only did Clare not "outgrow" her conviction on these matters, she understood her advantage and knew how to leverage it. First, she understood how rapidly the female societies were proliferating and that they were doing so under the model she had forged when she made her bold dash from nobility to poverty. She followed Francis under a very specific mandate, and it was this model, along with the courage of her example, that ignited the imaginations of so many women whose spirits were enlivened with a similar hope. The pope needed her, in other words. He was intent upon consolidating the female reforming societies all over Italy and Europe and needed the validation of Clare's authority. So, in an odd way, though they stood in opposite corners of their respective designs for the women's houses, they each needed the aid of the other. Beyond Clare's shrewd leveraging of her station to win the desired exemption, she further unflinchingly stood on the authority of Francis, who had urged her and the Poor Sisters always to love and embrace poverty in the way of the Lord. Gregory IX, who had just canonized Francis, could hardly undermine the spiritual authority of the beloved saint, whose devoted followers he likewise needed to advance and stabilize his cause, particularly given his precarious political situation.

Gregory possessed a shrewdness of his own and did not hesitate in using it to gain an advantage in this delicate dance with Clare. Along with the "Privilege of Poverty" exemption he rendered to her and the

156 Mueller, *Privilege*, 40.

Poor Sisters at San Damiano, he also wrote a letter[157] accompanying it in which he appealed to Clare to reflect on how what seemed bitter to them then might, in time, become in their hearts something sweet. He was alluding to words Francis used in his "Testament" describing the change that came over him after embracing a leper: "And when I left them, what had seemed bitter to me was turned into sweetness of soul and body. And afterwards I delayed a little and left the world."[158] Gregory's appeal to Francis's change of heart could be seen by Clare as a low blow, since she and her sisters repeatedly appealed to their devotion to Francis's ideals as the sole authority on which they stood their ground. Essentially, Gregory was appealing to Francis's model of reversing himself to woo Clare with the same possibility.

The tactic did not work. So, while given a temporary reprieve with her standard of poverty, the tug of war between the pope and Clare was hardly resolved. More and more female monasteries were popping up all over Italy and in Europe. The Franciscan movement was exploding, and, for this short season, Clare and Gregory IX each held differing ends of the rope in unresolved tension that would determine which way this movement would go.

---

157 "Letter of Pope Gregory IX" (1228), *CA:ED*, 131.
158 "Testament" (1226), *FA:ED*, vol. 1, 124.

CHAPTER 7

LETTERS

lare's most acclaimed and endeared ally in the cause of preserving Franciscan poverty came in the person of Agnes of Prague, a young woman of royal lineage from Bohemia. Agnes, a protege of Clare's, became a strategic and inviolable ally for establishing and preserving Clare's vision for Franciscan female societies in Europe, even as Gregory IX waged his campaign to define women's monasteries under the Benedictine model. Clare called Agnes "the other half of my soul and one held most dear."[159]

Agnes was almost twenty years younger than Clare, born in 1211, the youngest of nine children of King Premysl Otakar I of Bohemia and Queen Constance of Hungary.[160] Like Clare's mother, Ortolana, Agnes's mother, Constance, was a devoted Christian and a generous benefactor of local churches and cloisters. Like Clare's father, Favorone, Agnes's father, Otakar, undertook to arrange a strategic marriage for his daughter when she was very young. In 1219, when Agnes was eight and when Clare would have been in her mid-twenties, Emperor Frederick II approached Otakar with the intention of securing a marriage alliance between Agnes and his son Henry, who at the age of 10 had just been crowned King of Germany. Otakar welcomed the plan and promptly undertook grooming the young Agnes for regal life

---

159 4LAg, 1.
160 Constance was his second marriage, and he rendered the rights of succession to her offspring, disregarding those rights of the four children he shared with his first wife, Adele.

as the soon-to-be queen of Germany. To that end, in 1220 he sent his young daughter to the Court of Leopold VI, the Austrian Babenburger duke, for the appropriate care and oversight. Leopold, however, saw the advantage of a marriage into the powerful German family and sabotaged the arrangement. He appealed to the pope—then Honorius III—and began negotiating terms of betrothal of his daughter, Margaret of Austria, to Frederick's son Henry. Leopold presented the papal approval to Frederick, who promptly abandoned Agnes after a six-year betrothal while turning his intentions to Margaret, securing a marriage for Henry.

As was fitting for the age, Otakar then, in 1226, went to war against Austria and Leopold in retribution. The Bohemian king was decisively defeated but, regardless, persisted in his designs until the summons arose for fighting men to join the Sixth Crusade. This emptied the reservoir of combatants and overthrew his plan to exact revenge on Leopold. Otakar died a few years later, in 1230, never gaining his satisfaction. His son Wenceslas then ascended to his father's throne and would prove a powerful ally to the religious cause of his beloved sister, Agnes. In the meantime, Frederick II still deemed it expedient to secure an alliance with the Bohemians and adapted his strategy accordingly. In 1231 Frederick broached Wenceslas, presenting himself as a suitor for Agnes's hand in marriage.

Agnes had already determined that she did not want to marry Frederick II or anyone else, sensing a strong pull toward a life of penance and poverty. She appealed to none other than Pope Gregory IX regarding the predicament, asking to be taken under his care as a spiritual daughter, which would effectively remove her from contention in the realm of royal marriage. Gregory was more than happy to grant her request, ready as he was always to foil the political strategies of Emperor Frederick II. It further helped her cause that Agnes's brother was a king who loved her and supported her religious leanings. Agnes informed Wenceslas of her intentions not to marry and showed him the validating papal blessing. In a show of familial affection, Wenceslas granted her request not to marry Frederick, though he feared the political repercussions of what inevitably would be an embarrassment.

Here we see another glimpse of the basic humanity of these larger-than-life political champions. Frederick accepted Agnes's rebuff humbly: "If this offense had been committed against us by any man, under no circumstances would we refrain from avenging the insult of such contempt. However, because she has chosen a Lord who is greater than we are, we do not consider this to be any insult against us. Instead, we believe that this action has been inspired by God."[161]

A singular event occurred that same year which decisively shaped Agnes's destiny: the death of her cousin, Elizabeth of Thuringia (Hungary). Elizabeth was four years older than her cousin and, like Agnes, was the sister of a king—in this case, the king of Hungary. Elizabeth had been inspired by the preaching of Franciscan brothers she had heard in Germany in 1220. And while a life of gospel poverty appealed to her, she had been betrothed to Louis IV of Thuringia and married him in 1221 at the age of 14. She bore him three children. Louis died of the plague a few years later, in 1227, while en route to fight in a crusade. This left the grief-stricken Elizabeth alone and abandoned by the family members of her husband's royal court. She remembered the Franciscan brothers, whose lives and words had left so great an impression on her, and the year following her husband's death she took the vows of a Third-Order Franciscan.[162] She secured the care of her children in the royal household, renounced her rank, and used her widow's pension to found a hospital for

---

161 *Legend of Agnes* 2:2; The *Legend* is quoted from Mueller, The *Privilege of Poverty*, who is citing the translation of Jan Kapistrán Vyskočil. *Legenda blahoslavené Anežky a čtyri listy sv.* Kláry. Prague: Nakladatelství Universum, 1932. All subsequent references to the *Legend of Agnes* come from this version.

162 Third Order Franciscans are also called the SFO—Secular Franciscan Order, created in 1221 by Francis to accommodate brothers and sisters of the penitential movement who wished to live by the Order's convictions but were prevented from joining because of marriage or other ties.

the poor in Marburg. Amid harsh living conditions and other hardships, Elizabeth succumbed to illness a few years later in 1231 and died at the age of 24.[163]

Agnes was 20 when her cousin died, and this affected her profoundly. Following Elizabeth's footsteps, Agnes too used her wealth to fund a similar hospital for the poor in Prague, dedicating it to Saint Francis. Her mother, Constance, endowed it with various estates for its perpetual sustenance. Beyond that, Agnes used her dowry to build a Franciscan monastery for women in Prague very near the hospital, welcoming five sisters from Trent who had come to Prague for the purpose of becoming its founding members. Shortly after that, in November 1233, seven more noblewomen from Bohemia joined. Agnes entered the monastery in June 1234.[164]

Gregory IX wrote to congratulate her on her new life as a religious, comparing her to the well-known virgin martyr Agnes of Rome:

> Despite your charm and youth, Agnes, you imitated the most blessed Agnes.[165] Like her, you did not permit yourself to be deceived by worldly pleasantries or seduced by temporal power or glory. Rather, despising the enticements of the world and the

---

163 Elizabeth of Hungary was canonized by Pope Gregory IX in 1235, with the support of Frederick II. For the next few centuries Elizabeth became one of "the most popular female saints in Europe during the thirteenth and fourteenth centuries, and many wealthy women emulated her" (Mueller, *Privilege*, 55). She was hailed by the church hierarchy for her loyalty to Mother Church and equally hailed by reformers and dissenters for her devotion to Franciscan ideals.

164 Noted in the 13th-century document the *Annales Stadenses*: "In the same year on the day of Pentecost, at the request of the Friars Minor, the sister of the king of Bohemia, Lady Agnes, gave herself to the Order of Poor Ladies of the Rule of Blessed Francis in Prague. She did so having, on account of Christ, rejected Emperor Frederick, who had previously asked her to marry him" *Annales Stadenses*, 363.

165 Agnes of Rome (c. 291– c. 304): A beautiful young girl of wealthy family, Agnes had many suitors of high rank, and the young men, slighted by her resolute devotion to religious purity, submitted her name to the authorities as a follower of Christianity. The Prefect Sempronius ordered her to be dragged naked through the streets to a brothel. At her trial she was sentenced to death and led out to be burned at the stake, though tradition says the wood would not burn. Instead the officer in charge drew his sword and beheaded her, or in other texts, stabbed her in the throat.

riches of earthly affairs, you compelled the flesh to serve the spirit. In doing so, you left behind everything transitory, so that you might choose in purity of heart and body to serve your Heavenly Spouse in the religious community of Poor Enclosed Nuns.[166]

When Agnes joined the monastery she was 23 and Clare was in her early 40s. It was at this point that Clare initiated a correspondence with Agnes[167] that, more than any other source, offers a window into the political and practical realities facing the Franciscan movement at the time. More pointedly, the letters highlight Clare's highly developed spiritual vision and the theology behind her understanding of poverty. (This is examined in more detail in Chapter 8.)

First Letter

Clare's first letter to Agnes inaugurates what would become a long-standing bond between these two women of rank who, as if moved by a single soul, upheld the ideal of Franciscan poverty amid changing tides. She likely wrote the initial letter in the summer of 1234 upon hearing the news from itinerate friars that a member of Bohemia's royal household had entered religious life as a Franciscan.[168]

The Franciscan brothers knew the journey well between Prague and Assisi. They made it often, as was in keeping with their mandate as mendicant preachers. The trip to Prague involved a northern trek of about 750 miles over the Alps. Agnes herself had learned of the Franciscan movement through the preaching of these traveling friars, and when the circumstances of her life were right, she made the decision to follow the Franciscan way of poverty. European royalty had its own track for spreading news, and the Franciscan communities shared

---

166 *BF (Bullarium Franciscanum*, 1-4. Edited by Joannis Sbaralea. Rome: Sacrae Congregationis de Propagando Fide, 1759–68. Note Gregory's use of the term "Poor Enclosed Nuns," which stands in stark contrast to Clare's preferred "Poor Sisters."

167 Agnes's letters to Clare have been lost. Clare's four letters to Agnes of Prague are included in their entirety in the Appendices of this book.

168 Agnes entered the Order on Pentecost Sunday, June 11, 1234.

regular communications one with another. So news of this noblewoman's decision would have quickly reached Clare, whose life intersected both worlds.

Agnes was several years younger than Clare, and the latter seems to have positioned her as the torchbearer who would carry the ideal of Franciscan poverty against the changing tides that were swiftly overrunning the development of the Order in Europe and elsewhere. When Clare heard about Agnes's dramatic choice to renounce her royal station and embrace poverty—the kind of poverty that eschews all security and protections—she was keen to impart to Agnes the benefit of her wisdom and experience while simultaneously conferring to her a mandate. Clare was concerned that Agnes, right from the start, establish herself firmly in the Franciscan life—especially since Agnes, like Clare, contended with pressure from Gregory IX to change women's Orders.

A few salient points within the first letter reveal Clare's interest in clarifying for Agnes the true nature of her radical choice.[169] She draws a clear line of demarcation between what Agnes gained in the light of all she gave up. And again, we meet the illustrious Frederick II, who would crop up yet again in Clare's story.

> I rejoice because you, more than others—having the opportunity to become legitimately married with eminent glory to the illustrious emperor [Frederick II] as would befit your and his preeminence—could have enjoyed public ostentation, honors, and worldly status. Spurning all these things with your whole heart and mind, you have chosen instead holiest poverty and physical want, accepting a nobler spouse, the Lord Jesus Christ.[170]

Clare immediately located the heart of the matter regarding what it meant for Agnes to embrace Franciscan poverty. Agnes had been given

---

169 The four letters from Clare to Agnes can be seen in their entirety in the Appendix.
170 *LAg*, 5–6; *CA:ED*, 43.

the opportunity to be the wife of the Holy Roman Emperor—a worldly station unsurpassed in glory and privilege. The Franciscan way, however, always works itself out in real life and is not abstract. It meant that when Agnes chose a "nobler spouse," she did not do so only in her mind. She could not "marry Christ" and be the wife of the Emperor in the context of Franciscan piety. The choice carried practical consequences. Agnes gave up the pinnacle of human prestige to betroth herself to the "nobler spouse," which meant for her utter poverty. And Clare, in this first letter, is reassuring her that the terms of her betrothal are inviolable and of greater worth than any worldly station.

This letter introduces a theme that looms large in Clare's spiritual vision: the notion of Bridal Mysticism and the Great Exchange.[171] She quotes extensively from a document that was well-known among the women of the Middle Ages, the *Legend of Agnes of Rome*: "His power is stronger, his nobility higher, his appearance lovelier, his love sweeter and his every grace more elegant. You are now held tightly in the embrace of the one who has adorned your breast with precious stones and has hung priceless pearls from your ears."[172]

Beyond betrothal to a Heavenly Spouse, Clare affirms for Agnes in this letter that Franciscan poverty always returns to its beginning point, the poverty that Jesus himself knew. The Franciscans always return to Jesus; he is their plumb line. This is why, over the years of Francis's understanding of poverty being modified and tempered, Clare—and Francis, when he was alive—fought so fiercely to resist accommodating such changes. Clare helps Agnes stand in this truth: "Be strengthened in the holy service begun in you out of a burning desire for the Poor Crucified":

[C]ontempt of the world has pleased you more than its honors; poverty more than temporal riches; and storing up treasures in

---

171 This is discussed in more detail in chapter 8.
172 *1LAg*, 9– 10; *CA:ED*, 44.

heaven rather than on earth. . . . For I am sure that you know that the kingdom of heaven is promised and given by the Lord only to the poor, because—as long as something temporal is the object of love, the fruit of charity is lost. You know too that a person cannot serve God and material wealth [and] . . . that a person wearing clothing cannot fight with another who is naked, because the one who has something that might be grasped is more quickly thrown to the ground. . . . It is indeed a great and praiseworthy exchange to give up the temporal for the eternal.[173]

From her own place of poverty, Clare concludes the first letter with a humble solicitation for prayer: "I also beseech you in the Lord, as best as I can, to be so kind as to include in your most holy prayers me, your servant, although useless—and the other sisters who are devoted to you who live with me in the monastery."[174]

Second Letter

By the time of Clare's second letter to Agnes, sometime in 1235, Pope Gregory's machinations were causing Agnes great affliction. She was trying to gain a foothold in her monastery for the Franciscan model of devotion while Gregory continued to press his will. We already know that Gregory had specific plans for women's monasteries and that "the Franciscan model" was not part of those plans. In 1235 he sent Agnes a letter informing her that he was uniting as a single entity her monastery and the neighboring hospital that she and her mother had endowed. His design served as a backhanded way to force the monastery to accept the security of the endowments that had been established when the hospital was built. The money supporting the hospital would likewise benefit and undergird the monastery. This violated Agnes's intention for both.

---

173 *1LAg*, 22–30; *CA:ED* 45–46.
174 *1LAg*, 33; *CA:ED* 46.

Agnes wrote Clare, the foremost expert in contending with Pope Gregory IX, asking for guidance on how to navigate the situation. Clare's second letter is her response and, of all the letters, it offers a shimmering vision into the lucidity of Clare's mind. It shows her tenacity, her courage, her resolve, and her humility. Most pointedly, it speaks to her devotion and paints a picture of her uncompromising theology of poverty. That the letter is so short, yet so deep and lucid, is a testament to Clare's skills as a writer and the expansiveness and coherence of her thinking. This letter, more than the others, also offers a glimpse into the beauty and sheer force of Clare's will.

> ... [B]e mindful of your commitment like another Rachel, always seeing your beginning. What you hold, may you hold. What you do, do and do not stop. But with swift pace, light step, unswerving feet, so that even your steps stir up no dust, may you go forward securely, joyfully, and swiftly, on the path of prudent happiness, believing nothing, agreeing with nothing that would dissuade you from this commitment or would place a stumbling block for you on the way, so that nothing prevents you from offering your vows to the Most High in the perfection to which the Spirit of the Lord has called you.

> ... If anyone has said anything else to you or suggested any other thing to you that might hinder your perfection or that would seem contrary to your divine vocation, even though you must respect him, do not follow his counsel.[175]

Clare is encouraging Agnes to defy the pope. When she urges her to "always see your beginning," she is reminding Agnes always to return to the poor crucified Christ. The "beginning" is the plumb line from which all other points are measured. The beginning, for Clare, is the poverty

175 *2LAg; CA:ED*, 48.

of Christ; anything that pulls Agnes away from that epicenter is to be decisively rebuffed. Once established on that solid ground, the rest, for Clare, is mere execution. "What you hold, hold; what you do, do." Clare exhorts Agnes to remember her vocation. That is her singular calling given by God, which carries his imprimatur and that alone is her duty. She is to execute it actively, consistently, unrelentingly, and with prudent happiness and a light step. Stay positive. Remain hopeful. Dismiss anything that would pull you off course, even if it is the pope himself who attempts to dissuade you. Do not agree. Look only to the Most High (not the pope) for the perfection you seek. Show respect, but do not follow any counsel that is contrary to your singular vocation. In practical terms, Clare urges Agnes not to follow the counsel of the pope, but to do so respectfully.

Third Letter

The third letter Clare wrote to Agnes, probably in the summer of 1238, shows that Agnes was winning a major battle in her tug of war with Pope Gregory IX, yet was still contending with inner turmoil and especially anger about his contrivances. As a gesture of appeasement, Gregory had conferred to Agnes the same special exemption of the "Privilege of Poverty" that he had given to Clare's monastery at San Damiano. It was a concession he made in exchange for gaining political advantage with Agnes's brother, King Wenceslas, who at this point had assumed the throne of King of Bohemia. (Agnes's brother's being king would avail her many advantages.) Gregory's heart wasn't in the exemption, and when Agnes further petitioned him to allow her monastery to adopt a Franciscan Rule instead of the Benedictine Rule that he'd imposed upon all the female monasteries in Europe, Gregory rebuffed her. He maintained that adopting the Benedictine Rule was part of the deal in his rendering the exemption of poverty, and it irked him that he had to remind her of that.

Clare wrote her letter to settle Agnes and to help her steady herself, while standing firm in the victory she had won. She encouraged Agnes to be resolute, fixing her eyes on higher vistas, and not to get tripped up with the unrelenting antagonisms of Gregory. In Clare's third letter she advises Agnes to look in the mirror and see herself as the bejeweled spouse of the Divine Husband. All her longings would be answered there. She calls Agnes to return to this first principle: to behold the beauty lavishly bestowed upon the bride by the Divine Husband. "May you totally love him who gave himself totally for your love, whose beauty the sun and the moon admire."[176]

> Truly I can rejoice, and no one can rob me of such joy, since, having at last what under heaven I have desired, I see that, helped by a special gift of wisdom from the mouth of God Himself and in an awe-inspiring and unexpected way, you have brought to ruin the subtleties of our crafty enemy, the pride that destroys human nature, and the vanity that infatuates human hearts; that by humility, the virtue of faith, and the arms of poverty, you have taken hold of that incomparable treasure hidden in the field of the world and of the human heart, with which you have purchased that by Whom all things have been made from nothing. . . .

> And may neither bitterness nor a cloud overwhelm you,
> O dearly beloved Lady in Christ,
> Joy of the angels and crown of your sisters!
> Place your mind before the mirror of eternity!
> Place your soul in the brilliance of glory!
> Place your heart in the figure of the divine substance
>   And, through contemplation,
> Transform your entire being into the image
> Of the Godhead Itself,
> So that you too may feel what friends feel
>   In tasting the hidden sweetness

176 *3LAg; CA:ED*, 51.

That, from the beginning,

God Himself has reserved for His lovers.

And, after all who ensnare their blind lovers

In a deceitful and turbulent world

Have been completely passed over,

May you totally love Him Who gave Himself totally for your love,

At Whose beauty the sun and the moon marvel,

Whose rewards and their uniqueness and grandeur have no limits.[177]

Fourth Letter

The fourth letter Clare wrote Agnes in 1253 would be her last, as she wrote it when she was near death. It was her final goodbye. It had been fifteen years since she had written Agnes, as far as the record shows. This was due, in part, to geopolitical instability, making travel by road, hence letter-delivery, especially hazardous. Few ventured to make such journeys, even among the Franciscans.[178] By this point in both Clare's life and Agnes's situation, there was no more advice to render regarding how to deal with popes and the political maneuverings that were changing the Franciscan Order. Pope Gregory had died in 1241, and his successor, Innocent IV, had picked up where Gregory left off when it came to securing the female monasteries under the Benedictine model. Even so, both Clare and Agnes had won the exemption of the "Privilege of Poverty," and Innocent did not attempt to overrule it. This final letter of Clare's effuses with affection and especially the high theology of gazing into the mirror that she had touched upon in the last one. At this point in Clare's waning life, the world inside the mirror was the world she inhabited.

---

177 3LAg, CA:ED, 50.

178 Clare explains in her letter: "Do not wonder at all or think that the fire of love for you glows with less delight in your mother's heart. No, this is the difficulty: the lack of messengers and the obvious dangers of the roads." 4LAg, 5–6.

Since He is the radiance of eternal glory,

is the brightness of eternal light and

the mirror without blemish,

Gaze upon that mirror each day,

O Queen and Spouse of Jesus Christ,

and continually study your face in it,

that you may adorn yourself completely,

within and without,

covered and arrayed in needlework

and similarly adorned

with the flowers and garments of all the virtues,

as is becoming, the daughter and dearest bride

of the Most High King.

Indeed, in that mirror,

blessed poverty, holy humility,

and inexpressible charity shine forth, with the grace of God,

as you will be able to contemplate them throughout

the entire mirror. . . .

Then reflect upon, at the surface of the mirror, the holy humility,

at least the blessed poverty, the untold labors and punishments

that He endured for the redemption of the whole human race.[179]

Agnes Carries On

Agnes would outlive Clare by almost three decades, and during that time she struggled. A little more than a month after Clare died, her beloved brother and protector, King Wenceslas—after a tumultuous reign wrought with discord and rebellion—died at the age of 48. These two losses, so close to one another, were especially devastating for Agnes personally and politically.

179 4LAg; CA:ED, 56.

After the death of her brother, the political landscape in Bohemia began to unravel, carrying repercussions for Agnes's already tenuous hold on Franciscan poverty for her monastery. During the years following Wenceslas's death, the sisters at the monastery in Prague were languishing because the instability of the times caused a lack of provisions. In the wake of a critical church council that was held in 1274, the Council of Lyons, and under the pontificate of Pope Gregory X (who again continued the effort to consolidate the various religious Orders, after Innocent IV), Cardinal John Cajetan urged Agnes to accept economic support due to "evils of the age and the threatening dangerous times."[180] Agnes rebuffed the idea: "She resisted with a courageous spirit, much preferring to be without anything, voluntarily accepting all want and destitution rather than to depart in any way from the poverty of Christ who became poor for our sake."[181]

Because of the political instability and the mismanagement of the crown by Wenceslas's successor—Agnes's nephew—the royal house was eventually vanquished and banished from Prague. By the end of her life, Agnes was the only blood member of the royal line to remain in Prague. And there she lived out her days.

She died during Lent on March 2, 1282, beloved by the people of Prague, and especially the poor, who knew better than anyone the true measure of her devotion. The one who washed their foul linens and tended their sick was the same one who should have been their queen.

---

180 *Legend of Agnes*, 5:1.
181 *Legend of Agnes*, 5:1.

||||||||||||||||||||||||||||||||||||||||||

CHAPTER 8

INTERIOR LANDSCAPE

T he previous chapter explored advice Clare gave to Agnes of Prague, lending a window into both her theology of poverty and of Bridal Mysticism. The latter was a common expression of penitential faith for women in the Middle Ages, and it is worth taking the time to explore these concepts in greater depth in order to gain a clearer understanding of the world Clare inhabited inside her mind.

Poverty

Many in today's modern world simply cannot fathom the idea that poverty, as embodied in the lives of Francis and Clare, could be deemed as blessed, and more, that it ought to be sought after. Having lived in Honduras many years ago, I confronted abject poverty every day, even as I went to the grocery store to purchase my sons' lunch snacks. There is nothing romantic about it. Poverty is gritty and dark and sorrowful and desperate. It can suck the life and soul out of you. People who are poor have no options, which means they often have no recourse or justice when they are wronged. Being poor turns one's face hard. It is difficult to wait in federal assistance lines and use loose change to purchase the week's necessities. I have struggled with the mindset of medieval penitents who uphold the notion that poverty ought to be embraced. I am not enamored of the idea of choosing poverty, as Clare did, along with many others who joined the male and female Franciscan Orders.

The writings of a particular female penitent who joined the Franciscans after Clare's death have proven helpful to me in understanding the spiritual nuances of the kind of poverty Clare and Francis embodied. Angela of Foligno is an outstanding example of the next generation of female penitents who strove to uphold Franciscan poverty after Clare's death. Angela never knew Clare; she was five when Clare died. But her life was radically touched by the Franciscan movement and particularly by Clare's spiritual vision. Prior to joining the Third Order Franciscans at about 40, Angela had spent the early years of her adult life seeking material wealth and wanton pleasure. She had been born into a wealthy Italian family and married a man of high social standing with whom she had several children. Even so, she continued to pursue social ambition and wealth, even to the point of engaging in adulterous relationships. At about 40, she experienced a dramatic conversion, owning her wanton pursuits and repenting of them in great sorrow. Tragedy then struck when her mother, husband, and children died. At this point, she sold all her worldly possessions and joined the Third Order Franciscans, founding a lay women's religious group to serve the poor and live a life of penance and humility.

Angela became a prolific writer and outlined Franciscan poverty in *The Book of Divine Consolation of the Blessed Angela of Foligno*[182] from which I highlight a few salient points.

Poverty produces self-reflection. Choosing a life of poverty, she asserts, enables a person to know herself and to know God. What one can endure and the spirit with which one endures it expose the measure of a human soul. Conversely, the desperation that may set in, being reduced to levels of utter dependency, drives the penitent to the heart of God. Then, crying out for help and sustenance and, receiving it, the penitent grows in God's graces.

Poverty offers grace. By confronting the corner of the heart that cries out in utter dependence, the penitent receives "grace upon grace, light

---

182 *The Book of Divine Consolation of the Blessed Angela of Foligno*, trans. Mary G. Steegmann, (London: Chatto and Windus, 1909).

upon light, and vision upon vision," and thereby comes to a more vibrant understanding of God. Angela says, "The better he is known, the more he loves, the more he loves the more powerfully he works."

Poverty fosters perfect humility and a willingness to be despised. This kind of thinking is alien to modern devotion—particularly American devotion—and in some circles it would even be considered self-destructive. In the context of the Middle Ages and its understanding of penance, the willingness to be despised meant only that one's complete satisfaction lay in being "cherished in the heart of none save of God alone, and by Him alone to be held in good repute." Francis is the foremost example of this kind of humility, as he was forever reminding his brothers of his own wretchedness. One of his brothers, Masseo, who was "a big man and handsome of body," once cried out to Francis, "You aren't a handsome man, you aren't someone of great learning, you're not noble. Why after you? Why after you? Why does all the world seem to be running after you and everyone seems to want to see you and hear you and obey you?" Francis responded:

> "Do you want to know why after me? You want to know why the whole world comes after me? I have this from those eyes of the Most High God, which gaze in every place on the good and the guilty. Since those most holy eyes have not seen among sinners anyone more vile, nor more incompetent, nor a greater sinner than me; to perform that marvelous work, which he intends to do, He has not found a more vile creature on the earth, and therefore He has chosen me."[183]

Poverty strengthens human will to remain resolute in one's utter devotion in following the way of Jesus. That means—as Clare noted in her letter to Agnes—rebuffing, rebuking, or fleeing anything or anyone who might thwart such devotion. Angela of Foligno echoed Clare: "[We] must

183 *Fioretti, FA:ED,* vol. 3, 587.

flee as though from a pestilence from all who hinder it from attaining these things, whether it be a carnal or spiritual person, and all the things of this world which it holds to be contrary to that good thing."

Poverty removes the tendency to judge others. When someone has attained this level of personal devotion—of denying oneself to follow in the footsteps of Jesus—it removes any tendency one might otherwise exert to judge others. "[He] pronounces no judgment upon any other creature whatsoever, nor seeks to judge others, as the Gospel says. [He] must esteem [himself] more vile than all others (howsoever evil they may be) and unworthy of the grace of God. It must know, moreover, that whosoever strives to possess [poverty and its associated suffering] in this present life and mortal struggle will possess God in fulness here after."[184]

On one level, these penitents understood that by taking the vow of poverty they were surrendering their lives to a position of powerlessness. There would be no options or recourse in the arena of power and privilege. Franciscan poverty meant living in a way that forced trust, not an abstract but a concrete trust. They utterly depended on the beneficence of their neighbors and the provision of God for day-to-day sustenance. So, on another level—let's call it the Franciscan level—though powerless, poverty put penitents in lockstep with the heart of Jesus and in that way rendered them a kind of untouchable power.

By taking the vow of poverty Clare and Francis disqualified themselves from the terms under which the world engaged, the game of wealth and property as the way to wield influence and control. They removed themselves from that arena; they were indebted to no one for anything; no one had any claim on them. This enabled them to carry an authority that no one could challenge, thwart, or undermine. They walked freely in the world, "naked"—as Clare put it in her first letter to Agnes—because they possessed nothing that might be grasped and cause them more easily to be thrown to the ground.

184 *Book of Divine Consolation*, ch. 38.

This is what Clare calls the divine exchange: "It is indeed a great and praiseworthy exchange to give up the temporal for the eternal." She uses the image of the mirror as the portal of the exchange. After shedding the vanities of the world she left behind, she shifts her gaze to behold the new world she now claims and she sees it in a mirror.

The Mirror and the Great Exchange

During the medieval period, though mirrors were rough-hewn, they were coming into wide usage. They carried an element of mystery, perhaps even magic, in the minds of many and were sometimes used for divination, a practice forbidden by the Church. Mirrors were mentioned in literary sources with regularity at this time, and the work of Brother Leo, Francis's beloved friend and amanuensis, is a case in point. He titled one of his key documents tracing the life of Francis *The Mirror of Perfection*, explaining the title at the document's conclusion: "Here ends the mirror of perfection of a brother mirror. The Blessed Francis, wherein we may most sufficiently behold, as in a glass the perfection of his calling and profession."[185]

The idea of interpreting one's life through the reflected image in a mirror as a religious exercise captured the imagination of many at that time. It proved a helpful tool for cultivating spiritual contemplation, particularly for women of rank who had given up royalty and nobility in exchange for penitence and poverty. Though living in poverty, gazing into a mirror animated the holy imagination of these women to picture themselves in a sacred marriage in union with Christ. And this, in an odd way, answered many unmet longings in these women's lives. In marriage to Christ, they could reclaim nobility, dignity, and majesty as they saw themselves as spouses of Christ himself. Clare wrote to Agnes to "place your mind in the mirror of eternity; place your soul in the splendor of glory; place your heart in the figure of the divine substance and into the image of the Divine One himself." The exercise held transformative

185 *MP; FA:ED*, vol. 3, 205.

power for both Agnes and Clare (and countless other female penitents) as Clare advised Agnes to see in her face the bejeweled spouse of the Divine Husband, "the King himself [who] will take you into the heavenly bridal chamber."

The mirror opened a vision of a sublime world for these women who left worldly vanities to betroth themselves to Christ. This showed itself in the feminine spiritual expression that came to be known as Bridal Mysticism, and Clare lived it and encouraged her sisters to live it.

Bridal Mysticism

Francis of Assisi ascribed to women an unprecedented place in his movement, and this impulse was shaped and elevated by Clare, especially as her role evolved after following Francis in poverty. Feminine Franciscan spirituality resonated with the penitential movement in the Middle Ages, since many women joined the movement as means of freeing themselves of the obligations and constraints of rank and class and, in so doing, forfeited marriage and having a family. In answer to natural feminine longings, many female contemplatives embraced Bridal Mysticism, also known as "love mysticism." The expression deemed the devoted follower as having a love affair with the soul of God expressed in bridal imagery drawn from the Song of Solomon. Clare's first letter hails Agnes as a bride festooned with adornments of her beloved: "He has adorned your breast with precious stones and placed his priceless pearls on your ears." Clare addresses unmet desire, attesting that there is no shame in yearning. It is good, she says, since such desire is planted into the human heart by God. True unmet longing is a desire for the experience of God. When the bride has reduced herself to poverty, only then is she unconstrained to rise and meet her Holy Groom. He crowns her with precious stones and places "blossoms of springtime on [her] head, a golden crown as a sign of holiness."

The love of the bride for the Heavenly Spouse, if authentic, will show itself in a variety of ways. This love, in the context of bridal devotion, means that the bride will abandon all forms of life save those which embody the form of life of her Beloved. This, inevitably, will result in difficulty and often rejection by the world she once embraced. Nonetheless, true devotion to the Beloved Spouse shows itself in the "forsaking all others and taking only him unto herself." The women who embraced this bridal spiritual vision have left the world of status and power and incurred its contempt. This contempt reduces them to a kind of humility that such a choice inevitably requires. But this devotion and this humility is the way of life of their Beloved Spouse.

This kind of love also exercises inner discipline and exertions of the mind and heart in devotion to the Beloved Husband until the bride assumes the same traits that reflect his nature: love of all creatures, humility, and gentility, such as are modeled in Jesus's interactions with outcasts, the rejected and castoffs, and even his disciples.

If this same bridal love remains steadfast in the pursuit of the love of the Beloved, it achieves the inevitable result of being wholly transformed by God: "Then do we no longer live in ourselves, but in Him . . . I pray you, keep control over yourselves and give not yourselves unto any creature, neither lend yourselves whatsoever; but give yourselves wholly to Him who says, 'Thou shalt love the Lord with all thine heart, and with all thy mind, and with all thy soul, and with all the strength that thou hast.'"

This complete transformation of the bride, who has left all to be betrothed to the Heavenly Spouse, is comparable to Jesus's description of what it takes to enter the kingdom: "The kingdom of heaven is like a merchant looking for fine pearls. When he found one of great value, he went away and sold everything he had and bought it" (Matt. 13:45–46). There is only one pearl and it is of inestimable value. To attain it requires an all-or-nothing response. This is the essence of Bridal Mysticism.

It's a love that submits the self's will to the will of the Beloved.

It's a love that strives to become like the Beloved. "If the Beloved is poor, she strives to be poor; if the Beloved be reputed as vile, then she seeks to be vile also; if the beloved is in grief, she seeks to be a sharer of that woe, in order that the condition of one may be like unto that of the other."[186]

These are confusing notions for the twenty-first-century mind. But the twenty-first-century mind is not the standard-bearer for the measure of true gospel devotion particularly as it was exhibited in the Middle Ages and especially as expressed in the language of spiritual betrothal.

Penance and Holy Tribulation

Although primary features of Bridal Mysticism were marked by singular devotion and betrothal to the heavenly Spouse, another element was essential to the inward life of the betrothed: the practice of penance. Doing penance was integral to the reforming monastic orders in the Middle Ages which were known as the *Ordo Poenitentium*—the Order of Penitents. It likewise was a strong component in feminine spirituality, carrying a self-reflective aspect that went beyond beholding the visage of the spouse of a Holy Husband. It is evidenced in a humble deferential submission to inevitable trials that would attend this union as part of the intimate communion with Jesus, who himself bore great suffering for us.

Accepting trials and perceiving them as a means to draw near to Christ, and pondering his sufferings enabled the penitent to derive the inherent benefits of "holy tribulation." Insofar as was possible, the penitent ought not to betray in public the weight of trials one was enduring, nor cease from day-to-day obligations. Doing penance was an invisible work pressing in on the soul even while daily duties had to be met graciously and, if possible, cheerfully. Tribulations "make us to grow," even if we do not perceive it. Angela of Foligno likened tribulations to the kind of growth that attends a garden: "Just as good earth, well prepared, puts forth shoots and bears fruit when the rain falls upon it, so does the soul grow in virtue when tribulation comes upon it."

186 From *Divine Consolation*, ch. 38.

It takes many ingredients to make a garden grow: healthy soil, sunshine, nutrients, and time. Yet without water all of these would be for naught—in fact, these otherwise necessary elements could actually become the vehicles through which a garden could shrivel up and die if it did not have the element of water to cause them to energize and work wholesomely for the life of the plant. Plants need water, which suggests that—if Angela's analogy holds—tribulations will be many, but are life-giving and necessary for the proper development of a human soul. Finally, tribulation "gives peace, comfort, rest, and calm."[187] It is true that once the dross is burned away in a human soul the distractions and petty temptations of everyday life lose their hold. If you've suffered some kind of devastating loss or are experiencing acute mental or emotional pain, you become almost incapable of feeling animated about matters that are superficial. This is a mark of holiness, and holiness means you are near to the heart of God.

Finally, tribulations were seen to "convert us unto God and, being converted, draw us more nigh unto Him." Or, to borrow from the great twentieth-century Anglican writer C. S. Lewis, "Pain insists upon being attended to. God whispers to us in our pleasures, speaks in our consciences, but shouts in our pains. It is his megaphone to rouse a deaf world."[188] Tribulations drive us to the bosom of our Father.

In the midst of Agnes's trials, Clare wrote: "[O]ne thing is necessary [and] I invoke this one thing and advise you, by the love of him to whom you have offered yourself as a holy and pleasing sacrifice: be mindful of your founding purpose, always seeing your beginning." Clare's exhortation to "always see your beginning" enjoins Agnes always to remember the beginning of her life as a penitent and the course she chose when forsaking her worldly destiny. Clare reminds her that dismissing her old life is the beginning of her *true* life, though it may be attended by scorn, dismissals, trials, and losing worldly glory. It is the beginning of

---

187 From *Divine Consolation*, ch. 38.
188 C. S. Lewis, *The Problem of Pain* (San Francisco: HarperOne, 1996), 91.

the sacred transaction through which God's graces are unleashed. Holy tribulations will attend the soul that unites to God through Christ. But when trials do their work and when the snares of worldly glory no longer hold sway, that which is true, free, and light-filled enters in and expands the soul, and life and everything in it.

In all these aspects, bridal mysticism gave expression to longings of many women of the Middle Ages who left their stations in life to follow Christ. Such mysticism was not the only way to enter such a union with God, but it was Clare's way. It was appropriated by her unique disposition and was befitting of her times.

CHAPTER 9

"THE TENOR OF OUR LIFE"

O f the papal documents that sought to dictate Clare's way of life there seemed to be no end. But in this chapter, the focus turns to Clare herself and the way she envisioned and executed the day-to-day way of life for her sisters as fashioned in her self-written "Form of Life," or Rule.[189]

To modern sensibilities, the lives these cloistered women lived seem shockingly constrained and deprived. One is left to wonder—why did these revolutionary female reformers choose to live like this? What good came of it? What was the point?

Clare appreciated such questions and insisted that anyone desiring to live her way of life and enter into the fellowship of the Poor Sisters must first be made aware to the fullest extent possible of "the tenor" of it. The key points that defined Clare's and her sisters' daily lives inside the cloister, as articulated in her "Form of Life," included the role of poverty, attire, fasting, and the authority of the abbess and prayer. Each is examined briefly, one at a time.

Poverty

The foremost element for Clare in her "Form of Life," was the place of poverty. She says that the words of Jesus in the Gospel must be summoned

---

189 *FLCl*, 2:6; the elements included here are taken from Clare's *Form of Life*, which was confirmed in 1253 when Clare was on her death bed. Though it had not been the official document of the Order during Clare's life, it nevertheless creates a clear picture of the way Clare lived and operated as abbess, and the principles she lived by and made official when her *Form of Life* was finally approved by Pope Innocent IV.

wherein he asserts that those who desire to follow him must sell their possessions and distribute the proceeds to the poor.[190] What is important to glean is the nuance Clare brings to this otherwise unbending stricture. She tempers it to accommodate individual circumstances: "If she cannot do this, her good will shall suffice."[191] She further exhorts the sisters not to concern themselves overmuch with the "temporal affairs" of the novice "so that she may freely dispose of her possessions as the Lord shall have inspired."[192]

Attire

Once the novice has been accepted, a year of probation commences with the outward mark of the tonsure, such as Francis bestowed upon Clare the night she fled her family to follow him. After "her hair has been cut all around," Clare writes, the novice is permitted to have three tunics and a mantle. The tonsure signifies her consecration while the tunic signifies penance.[193] Clare leaves to the discretion of the abbess to "provide them with clothing according to the diversity of personal places, seasons and cold climates,"[194] though she was austere in her choice of garments: "She was also so severe toward her body that she was content with only one tunic of *lazzo* and one mantle. If she ever saw that the tunic of another of the sisters was worse than what she was wearing, she took it from her for herself and gave the better one to that sister. . . . She also said she used such rough haircloths and shirts for herself, but was very merciful to the sisters who could not endure such harshness and willingly gave them consolation."[195]

And so the novice embarks on her life inside the cloister, though even here Clare offers flexibility: "She may not go outside the monastery

190 Matthew 19:21.
191 *FLCl*, 2:8; *CA:ED*, 110.
192 *FLCl*, 6:9; *CA:ED*, 118.
193 *FLCl*, *CA:ED*, 111, note c.
194 *FLCl*, 2:16; *CA:ED*, 110.
195 *PC* 2 and 4; *CA:ED* 150 and 162.

except for a useful, reasonable, evident and justifiable purpose."[196] She also makes an exception for those sisters "who serve outside the monastery," to whom Clare also gives permission to wear shoes.[197] Since Franciscan poverty depends upon the sisters making their own way, with significant help from the friars, the survival of the Order depended upon their ability to conduct business. Clare sewed altar linens and mantels for local churches.[198] The contingency to allow some sisters freedom to leave the cloister in order to support the others attests to Clare's acumen, both practically and pastorally. Both Pope Gregory IX and Pope Innocent IV, in their Forms of Life, had pressured Clare to accept provisions from dowries in order to keep the monastery solvent without the women having to work; this would have tightened the parameters of the cloister, which Clare strongly opposed.

Fasting

Clare's disposition toward fasting is, for me, one of the most peculiar facets of her otherwise grace-filled spiritual vision. Fasting as a discipline generally was almost universally practiced in the various penitential reform movements that marked the Middle Ages. One way of seeing it would be to liken it to the bodily version of the discipline of poverty. While voluntary poverty worked as a kind of inoculant against the corruptions and temptations of the world, fasting could be understood as a preemptive strike against the lures of the flesh and unharnessed appetites. Penitents further believed, as Jesus proclaimed, that fasting carried great spiritual power that could be summoned to defeat the wiles of the devil. Beyond

---

196 *PC*, 2:12; *CA:ED*, 152.

197 *PC* 2:21-22; *CA:ED*, 154-155.

198 *PC* 1, 11: "She also said that when she was so sick that she could not get up from bed, she had herself raised to sit up and be supported with some cushions behind her back. She spun [thread] so from her work she made corporals and altar linens for almost all the churches of the plains and hills around Assisi. Asked how she knew these things, she replied that she saw her spinning. When the cloth was made and the sisters had sewn it, it was hand-delivered by the brothers to those churches and given to the priests who came there. (Sister Pacifica de Guelfuccio of Assisi, First Witness). *CA:ED*, 147.

fasting as a spiritual exercise, for Clare's Order, regular fasting also kept the need for begging for alms at a manageable level.

She laid out the regimen for fasting: "Let the sisters fast at all times. They may eat twice on the Nativity of the Lord, however, no matter on what day it happens to fall."[199] For Clare, the fast consisted of a few pieces of bread and water or wine. She went farther than even this, as noted by a witness in the *Process*:

> Blessed Clare, before she was sick, practiced great abstinence: the greater Lent, of Saint Martin, she always fasted on bread and water, except on Sundays when she drank a little wine when there was some. Three days a week, Monday, Wednesday and Friday, she did not eat anything until that time when Saint Francis commanded her, in some way, to eat a little bit every day. Then, in order to practice obedience, she took a little bread and water. Asked how she knew this, she said she had seen her and she was present when Saint Francis made that command.[200]

Francis had to intervene and order Clare to take more food, which she was duty-bound to obey. Despite the harsh regimen for fasting, in her typical style, Clare always extended grace to those who were weak or young: "The younger sisters, those who are weak, and those who are serving outside the monastery may be mercifully dispensed as the abbess sees fit. But let the sisters not be bound to corporal fasting in time of manifest necessity."[201]

Abbess

Clare's profile of the role of abbess offers a clear glimpse into her understanding of *her* role in this capacity, remembering that she fought

199 *FLCl* 3: 8; *CA:ED*, 113.
200 *PC* 2,8; *CA:ED*, 151.
201 *FLCl* 3:10–11; *CA:ED* 113.

tooth-and-claw against Francis's decision to confer it upon her. She inevitably had to accept it, under obedience, but in so doing, she made it her own in defiance (when need be) of standard protocols.

The role of the abbess was, at that time, typically understood and embodied as one of power and privilege,[202] sometimes even politically but certainly ecclesiastically. Once Clare had surrendered her course to taking on this role, she reversed its standard protocols and turned it upside-down, very much in the way Francis turned upside-down the role of his Order in the larger landscape of the Church. Rather than assume the posture of authority that marked the position, she quickly established a new dynamic of equanimity. This is notable, for example, early in her "Form of Life," or Rule, when she discussed receiving a new sister into the Order: "If anyone should come to us desiring to accept this life, the abbess is bound to seek the consent of all the sisters; and if the majority have agreed, she may receive her."[203] The abbess was unable to make a unilateral decision, but was bound by the consensus of the sisters. The same was true in the election of an abbess. She was to bring "legal precision with insistence on a spirit of mutual responsibility of all members."[204]

In typical Franciscan fashion she reverses the role, making the position of abbess one who serves, leads by example, and wins obedience by dint of devotion rather than intimidation. "Let her [the abbess] be the last refuge for those who are troubled, lest despair overcome the weak."[205] She sees the role as pastoral, not judicial, and she extends deference and humility, especially to the young, as is evident in her repartee with Agnes of Prague. When discussing matters of "welfare and the good of the monastery," she defers to the opinions of the younger members because "the Lord frequently reveals what is better to the youngest."[206]

202 See chapter 4.
203 *FLCl*, 2:1; *CA:ED*, 110.
204 *CA:ED*, 114; note a.
205 *FLCl*, 4:12; *CA:ED*, 114.
206 *FLCl*, 4:18; some have argued that the inclusion of "the youngest" was Clare's appropriation of a portion in St. Benedict's Rule that uses in the same context the term "the least." *CA:ED* 115, note d.

Though silence was supposed to be kept between the prayer times known as Compline (night) and Terce (morning), and at meals, an exception was given to those who worked outside the monastery. In her role as abbess, Clare made other exceptions: "They may be permitted to speak with discernment in the infirmary for the recreation and service of the sick." Beyond that, she allows that the sisters may "always and everywhere communicate whatever is necessary briefly and in a quiet voice."[207]

The signature features of her identity as abbess were the grace and humility she brought to her role, never heavy-handed, always merciful, forever seeing the best in everyone in all contingencies.

Prayer

Praying the Divine Office marked the rhythm of the daily lives of the sisters. The Office included reading and reciting written prayers at regular intervals throughout the course of each day. These prayer times included Matins (pre-dawn), Lauds (sunrise), Prime (the first hour of the day, approximately 6 a.m.), Terce (the third hour, approximately 9 a.m.), Sext (the sixth hour, noon), None (mid-afternoon), Vespers (evening), and Compline (night). Of these offices, some were considered "major"— practiced devotedly—and others "minor"—practiced intermittently. Not all were practiced by all members of the community. Franciscans used a breviary—or prayer book—that denoted which prayers and canticles were recited on given days and at which times. In general, the readings included an opening antiphon (chant or song) and doxology, a hymn, a reading from the Psalms, another antiphon, reading from Scripture plus a response, a reading or canticle from the Gospel, a prayer, and dismissal. Interspersed additionally, depending upon the time of day and the Office being undertaken, would be recitation of the Our Father (the Lord's Prayer) and various intercessions.

---

207 *FLCl* 5:4; *CA:ED*, 115.

Clare emphasized the exercise of the liturgical life, as Francis did, as according to the dictum that came out of the Fourth Lateran Council of 1215 that said that liturgical practice would "overcome the negative effects of a deficient theology that was keeping the faithful from reception of the Eucharist due to an exaggerated sense of sin."[208] Praying, reading, and singing marked the rhythm of their days and no doubt could be heard resonating through the olive groves across the valley and into Assisi's city streets. The women in the monastery, if they did nothing else, permeated the life of their town, filling it with echoes of holiness as if sung by the mouths of angels.

Yet the question persists: What is the point of all this? Why would any woman, particularly a woman of rank in possession of worldly domains and powerful choices, choose instead a life that so stripped her of choices, so constrained and spartan—so pointless?

We've already noted the thrust of their beliefs: how they likened their vital role in a divine marriage. They divorced the world and its beguiling attachments in order to become the bejeweled bride of Christ, and in that union, to become the feminine manifestation of his grace. The rhythm of daily prayers, the simplicity of their attire, the dependency on provisions, the provenance of which they had no control, created in their humble habitation a refuge of trust, a sacred dwelling place for those otherwise wearied and broken by the brutalities of the world. They were a bellwether for God's faithfulness or, for lack of a better way of putting it, they were a holy presence.

The Franciscan claim on this world, if nothing else, came down to that. Franciscans were *present* and they embodied the presence of Jesus, the picture of whom had been lost through the years of church corruption and opulence. They were a light that rekindled the remembrance of

208 *CA:ED*, 113–114, note e.

Jesus and rekindled hope that he may again be found. The writer of a later document expounding on the life of Clare describes her and her community this way:

> Her heavenly realities became accessible to the eye of the mind. . . .
> Here a fragile sex, a defenseless assembly of women,
> while they mortify themselves and afflict their flesh,
> subdue the crowd of spirits and the tyrant of the underworld. . . .
> The fragile sex, burdened with the weight of the flesh,
> overcomes the powers of the air and turns back their deceits.[209]

A modern interpreter of these medieval religious reformers put it this way: "They limit themselves to living—preaching by work and by example—without wealth, without pomp, without legal rights, but not without force. . . . It would be a cruel injustice and ingratitude to pass by in silence the generations of indomitable laborers who had cleared the thorns from the souls of our fathers [and mothers] as they cleared the soil of Christian Europe."[210]

The simple sisters at San Damiano and the powerful presence of the humble Clare carried a significant impact on the town of Assisi and its inhabitants, as is seen in two fascinating historical events that found Clare and her sisters in the center of them.

---

209 *VL*, IX:8-10, 15, 20; *CA:ED*, 211.
210 Count Montalembert, *The Monks of the West, from Benedict to St. Bernard* (Boston: Thomas B. Noonan & Co., 1872), 3.

CHAPTER 10

ASSAULTS AND VISITS

T hough the externals of Clare's religious life were stark and constrained, and while she was confined to her bed unless she had ambulatory help, she found herself at the center of significant events that echoed the force of her presence and the degree of honor she commanded from those about her, simple and spare though her existence was.

In the 1240s, during the long time when Clare's letters to Agnes of Prague had temporarily subsided, the strife between papal and imperial powers escalated and bore down heavily in Central Italy, and Assisi especially. The power struggle between the two contemporary champions Gregory IX and Frederick II advanced unabated.

Frederick and his troops invaded Assisi twice within the span of a year, the first assault occurring in September of 1240. Frederick and Gregory had long been at odds, each antagonizing the other and both setting their sights on Assisi. Gregory was consolidating his power in the respective communes that still claimed loyalty to the pope, Assisi among them, while Frederick was determined to snatch this allegiance and convert these papal cities to imperial loyalty.

It was well-known that Gregory was strongly and intimately connected to the women's monastery below town, San Damiano, and that he possessed devoted fondness and respect for its leader, Clare. Frederick, too, had his eyes on Assisi for a number of reasons, not least his keen desire to antagonize Gregory. But beyond that, Assisi had been Frederick's place of birth[211] and his grandfather, Frederick of Barbarossa, had at one time taken residency in La Rocca, the high fortress overlooking the town. The grandson, Frederick II, wanted nothing more than to reclaim his hometown for the empire.

Frederick, being a military man, had traveled all over Europe and the Middle East in the effort to consolidate his power. His travels brought him into contact with the Saracen (Muslim) armies who were happy to assist the emperor, for a price, in his effort to overthrow the Church. So Frederick waged his campaigns with the military aid of warring Muslims who had earned their stripes in battles in the Crusades. They were mercenaries, in other words.

As Frederick's army advanced from the south, his mercenaries attacked and pillaged towns and monasteries along the way. They held nothing back in the effort to topple the pope's control. On a Friday morning in September 1240, after having left a path of destruction along the way, the army fell upon Clare's peaceful monastery at San Damiano.

The Saracens disregarded protocols regarding the sacred nature of the female cloister. They climbed the walls and dropped to the other side to enter the premises with shields flinging and clanging swords. The sisters were understandably terrified. Clare took charge. Though she was immobile, she showed no visible fear, asking two sisters to carry her out to face the encroaching militants. She further ordered the sisters to retrieve the small "casket" that held the elements of the Eucharist. She held high the casket between them and the approaching warriors and importuned God for his favor. She heard a voice speak to her, in the way that many in the Middle Ages heard God's voice speak: "I will always defend you." Clare exhorted her sisters to trust in Christ, who defends them, and when she came into the presence of the Saracen army, they turned, retreated, and then fled.[212]

---

211 See ch. 1, note 24.
212 See Fortini/Moak, 362, note r.

This terrifying episode was recounted by Clare's sisters repeatedly in the testimonies on the *Process of Canonization*. Benvenuta of Perugia, who was the second witness in the *Process*, recounted, "Once, at the time of the war of Assisi, when certain Saracens scaled the wall and climbed down into the part within the cloister of San Damiano, our holy mother Saint Clare, then seriously ill, got up from her bed and called her sisters, comforting them not to be afraid. After she prayed, the Lord delivered the monastery and the sisters from the enemy. Those Saracens, who had just entered, departed."[213] The third witness, Sister Philippa, further noted, "She also said at the time of the war of Assisi the sisters were very much afraid of the arrival of those Tartars, Saracens, and other enemies of God and the Church. The blessed mother began to comfort them saying, 'My sisters and daughters, do not be afraid because, if the Lord is with us, the enemy cannot harm us. Have confidence in our Lord Jesus Christ because He will free us. I want to be your hostage so that you do not do anything bad. If they come, place me before them.'"[214] Sister Amata, who was the fourth witness, said, "[W]hen the sisters feared the arrival of the Saracens, Tartars, and other infidels, they asked the holy mother to do such with the Lord so the monastery would be protected from them. The holy mother responded: 'My sisters and daughters, do not fear because the Lord will defend you. I wish to be your ransom; if it should happen that the enemies come down to the monastery, place me before them.' Through the prayers of such a holy mother, the monastery, the sisters, and everything remained without a scratch."[215]

---

213 *PC* 2, 20; *CA:ED*, 154.
214 *PC*, 3:18; *CA:ED*, 159.
215 *PC*, 4,14. A footnote in *CA:ED, 154* points out that the attack upon San Damiano by the "Saracens," a band of Muslim soldiers of fortune or mercenaries in the pay of Frederick II (1210/15–1250), is one of the few incidents that can be dated with certainty: a Friday in September, 1240, at about the hour of Terce. What is curious, however, is that no historical record of this episode can be found. See Ezio Franceschini, "S. Chiara e i Saraceni," Chiara d'Assisi, Rassegna del Protomonastero, 1 (1953): 147–57; "I due asalti dei Saraceni a San Damiano e ad Assisi," Aevum XXVII (1953): 289–306.

Less than a year later, in the following June, a second assault was mounted against Assisi by the imperial army at the hands of a fierce military commander, Vitale d'Anversa, under Frederick's command. Having already wreaked havoc on the surrounding countryside, he encircled the city's perimeter and dug in. Vitale threatened to stay in position until he had successfully taken the city. When Clare heard of it, she instructed her sisters to pray: "From this city we receive every day many supplies. It would be impious if, where there is a need, we should not come to it in aid, according to our ability to do so."[216] During the night of June 21, she sprinkled ash on her head and gathered with the sisters in the small room known as the choir[217] to pray for the city. The next day, citizens of Assisi took up arms to repel the army and (for once) Assisi prevailed. The army retreated and the city was saved.[218]

Clare was at the center of another, more personal, incident a few years after these two assaults on the town. Though less dramatic in scale, the situation bespeaks the influence and trust she commanded from even those who did not know her, but who only knew of her.

While the cloistered sisters lived peaceably at the monastery below town, singing, praying, sewing, and gardening, the brutalities of the warring rival cities beyond their walls continued unabated. On one occasion a mercenary, soldier, and citizen of Assisi named Iacopo

---

216 Fortini/Moak, 362.

217 This room can still be seen at San Damiano as it existed during Clare's life.

218 The town commemorates this victory every year on June 22 with the Feast del Voto, when city and church officials, fraternities, and citizens make a procession to San Damiano the Basilica of Santa Chiara for ceremonies expressing the gratitude of the city for Clare and her prayers that secured the deliverance of the city. See Fortini/Moak, 362, note r.

di Stefano Presbitero joined a bloody skirmish between Assisi and neighboring Foligno. Iacopo's father, Stefano, had been a friend of Francis's during their youth and would have fought with him in the battles of Francis's early life. The son, Iacopo, had taken up arms as his father had, to defend Assisi against the unrelenting advance of Frederick and his imperial forces.

The battle was barbaric, and the *Assisiani* were routed in short order. The now-chastened Iacopo, having committed atrocities, grew reflective and pondered whether this terrible defeat was God's judgment for all the pillaging, looting, and assorted acts of violence he and others had carried out against the people of Foligno under the banner of the Church. He was overcome by guilt, and in his remorse wrote in his will that he desired to make amends to those whom he had harmed. War being warlike, he had lost trust in his companions and even in some of his family members when it came to assurances that his desires would be carried out. There was only one person he trusted to be true to his desire and whom he knew would faithfully execute the terms of his will: *dicta domina Sancte Damiani*—the one called the lady of San Damiano[219]—Clare. He named her co-executrix, with his brother, of his will, directing town officials to "proclaim publicly after his death that whoever had suffered wrongs done by him or his father or mother make claims for restitution upon his estate."[220] He further directed that whatever was left of his estate should go to the poor, and he left the fulfillment of these provisions in the hands of Clare.

Visits

Though the times were politically charged and tumultuous, and while the tenor of Francis's Order was changing, Clare found a refuge from it all during her frequent visits from Brother Leo, Francis's closest companion and champion. Leo visited Clare often, and together they

219 Fortini/Moak, 362.
220 Fortini/Moak, 364.

spent many hours reminiscing and collaborating on ways they could uphold Francis's mission amid the winds of change that conspired to alter it. Franciscan scholar Marco Bartoli describes this period in Clare's life: "[F]rom the time of Francis' death in 1226 until her own death in 1253, she transformed herself into a watchful witness of the blessed father's memory. . . . These same 27 years were also the most dramatic in the history of the Franciscan movement."[221]

During this period four major events occurred that drastically changed the direction of the Order: The building of the great basilica, which was undertaken in 1228; Francis's canonization by the newly elected Pope Gregory IX, Francis's friend; Francis's closest companions feeling increasingly alienated from the Order; and Pope Gregory IX issuing the papal decree called *Quo elongati*,[222] inaugurating the Order's transition from Francis's vision for the Order to a more conventional one—or from "intuition to institution."[223]

All of these events portended a shift that left Francis's original followers on the outside. When Pope Gregory IX started making plans for the erection of a great basilica in Assisi to be the permanent resting place of Francis's mortal remains, he also proceeded to collect money to pay for it. This scandalized those closest to Francis, who doggedly upheld the ideals of poverty espoused by their friend. Francis had objected to friars constructing any building for their use, and more so to their handling of money.[224] His closest friends considered the construction of the basilica

---

221 Bartoli, *Clare of Assisi, Beyond the Legend*, 104.

222 *Quo elongati* (September 28, 1230) was the first papal clarification of Francis's Rule introduced after Francis's death. "The pope broke the identification of Gospel and Rule with which Francis began his Rule . . . [and] declar[ed] that Francis's *Testament* was commendable but not binding in nature. . . . The document set aside Francis's dying wishes for his brothers [and] unleashed a debate about the obligation to the Gospel as their 'rule and life' and about the practice of poverty as its foundation. All of these discussions were no doubt aggravated by the building of the lavish basilica in honor of Saint Francis and, in 1232, the election of Brother Elias." *FA:ED*, vol. 1, 525.

223 *FA:ED*, vol. 1, Bartoli, 103.

224 He is known to have once climbed on the roof of a building under construction that he had believed to belong to the order and started tearing the roof off. *Legend of Perugia*, in *Omnibus*, vol. II, 987.

a betrayal of his ideals. The "little lamb" Leo is said to have taken a mallet to the marble collection box, an act for which he was soundly whipped and imprisoned.[225]

During this season of upheaval, the singular safe repository of the memory of Francis was San Damiano under the oversight of Clare. As Bartoli puts it, "diverse sources attribute to San Damiano this role of holding the memory [of Francis] and that they see Clare as the custodian of that memory."[226] So when in 1244 the Minister General of the Order, Crescentius of Iesi, summoned all living companions of Francis to document their memories of him, there is little doubt that Clare would have been part of this effort.

From the earliest days of my research, spanning well over a decade now, I have held in my thinking the notion that Clare was the unnamed author of a key early document composed in response to the 1244 summons. It was published under the names of three of Francis's closest companions, Leo, Angelo, and Rufino. Thus it has been called the *Legend of Three Companions*. A long tradition of controversy surrounds the origins of this document, and I do not presume to arbitrate the text-critical issues at work. I do, however, invite Franciscan scholars in the field to consider my thoughts on this point.

As I read *Three Companions* for the first time, I was struck not just by the intimate details presented in it, but the tone of the work. The most striking portion of the document that stood out to me, both in intimacy and tone, is the portion that details Francis's pre-conversion life—a period that even his earliest followers would not have known about without Francis directly conveying the information to them. And even if he did so, one is hard-pressed to consider that Francis would have included such nuance and intimate details when speaking of these matters to his brothers. The nature of the details involved personal matters related to

225 Omer Englebert, *Saint Francis of Assisi*, trans. Eve Marie Cooper (Chicago: Franciscan Herald Press, 1965), 158–159.
226 Bartoli, *Beyond the Legend*, 104.

the painful transition of Francis's life as he moved achingly from being the flamboyant extravagant playboy to the poor begging penitent.

The sensitivity with which the events of this difficult period are conveyed in *Legend of Three Companions* has the sound, to me, like the voice of a woman. And not just any woman's voice, but Clare's voice—a voice that, as we have already seen in her communications with Agnes of Prague and in her "Form of Life," is wise, intuitive, constrained, and grace-filled. I have already presented the possibility that Francis and Clare were in a relationship sooner than is typically assumed. I've also made the case that Clare was part of Francis's awakening to the religious life and that, from the start, he determined to include her in his life as a penitent. If my premise on these matters is true, then Clare would have been an eyewitness to the events described so poignantly and with such detail in this document relating to Francis's wrenching break from his family. After all, as his life turned to religion, he made his first priority— even before any thoughts of spearheading a new Order—to build a place for her to stay.

These are some of the intimate details regarding Francis's pre-conversion life:

He cut corners with some of his linens: "He was lavish, indeed prodigal, not only in these things, but also in spending more money on expensive clothes than his social position warranted. He was so vain in seeking to stand out that sometimes he had the most expensive material sewed together with the cheapest cloth onto the same garment" (1:2).

He spoke French badly: "Standing on the steps of the church with the other poor, he begged for alms in French, because he would speak French spontaneously, although he did not do so correctly" (3:9).

His lengthy conversion was tortured and had many twists: "He endured great suffering and mental anxiety, unable to rest until he accomplished in action what he had conceived in mind. Different thoughts followed one after the other, and their relentlessness disturbed him even more severely. For he was burning inwardly with a divine fire, unable to conceal outwardly the flame kindled in his soul. He repented that he had sinned so grievously. While his past and present transgressions no longer delighted him, he was not yet fully confident of refraining from future ones. This is why, when he emerged from the cave, he seemed to his companion to have changed into a different man" (4:12).

I simply cannot picture Francis conveying such intimate and nuanced texture to his male friends when (and if) he spoke to them of his early days.

Yet I can clearly hear Clare's voice in this narrative. The compassion shown in this narrative toward Francis's father—his harshest antagonist—is heartbreaking and clearly written from a heart that felt true compassion for his familial sorrow: "While he was staying there, his father, like a diligent spy, went around seeking to learn what might have happened to his son. And when he heard that he was so changed and was living in that place in such a way, he was touched inwardly with sorrow of heart and deeply disturbed by the sudden turn of events."[227]

Perhaps the most telling reason for my speculation, is the fact that the portion in *Three Companions* describing Francis's rebuilding San Damiano specifically to house women sounds nearly identical to Clare's description of the same event in her "Testament," including the use of the term "poor ladies" to denote the women of San Damiano (as opposed to "enclosed nuns," which was Pope Gregory IX's preferred term). It is also worth noting that Clare is never mentioned by name in the *Three Companions*. Its tone and cadence are similar to that which we find

227 *FA:ED*, 2, 78.

in Clare's letters to Agnes, and even the notion of Bridal Mysticism is alluded to in the narrative: "[His companions] asked him: 'What were you thinking about, that you did not follow us? Were you perhaps thinking about taking a wife?' He answered in an unequivocal voice: 'You are right! I was thinking about taking a wife more noble, wealthier, and more beautiful than you have ever seen.' They laughed at him. For he said this not of his own accord, but because he was inspired by God. In fact, the bride was the true religion that he later embraced, a bride more noble, richer and more beautiful because of her poverty."[228]

The portion of *Three Companions* that carries a notably differing tone is the portion describing Francis's death—an event that Clare would have missed because of her critical illness at the time.

The document is introduced by an opening letter, which carries the names of three of Francis's brothers who take credit for its authorship.[229] The letter serves as an Introduction, describing the purpose and content of their writing. Though the opening letter says one thing about the content of the document—that is not intended to be a "legend"—the body of the document says something else altogether—it is written as if it is a legend. These same three brothers remained close to Clare throughout the rest of her life, and two of them, Leo and Angelo, were present with her at her death. So it is plausible that they would have assisted her desire to have her say in answer to Crescentius's request for memories of Francis. This is especially true since, at this point of the textual tradition of recording the life of Francis, the presence and influence of Clare was beginning to be written out of the hagiographies. It is well-documented that those

---

228 *FA:ED*, 2, 72.

229 Some manuscripts (Foligno, Sarnano) begin the text of *L3C* with the following prologue: "Francis was seen to rise as a kind of new light, resplendent as the dawn and as the morning star, or even as the rising sun, setting the world alight, cleansing it, and giving it fertility. Like the sun, he shone by his words and works upon a world lying torpid amid winter's cold, darkness and sterility, lighting it up with radiant sparks, illuminating it with the rays of truth, and setting it afire with charity, renewing and embellishing it with the abundant fruit of his merits, and enriching it wonderfully with various fruit-bearing trees in the three Orders he founded. Thus did he bring the world to a kind of season of spring." *FA:ED*, vol. 2, 68.

closest to Francis deemed her the repository of Francis's memory, noted in the fact that when the tumult within the Order escalated, Leo left many of his manuscripts for safekeeping with Clare in San Damiano.[230] In the end, when the witnesses of Francis's life were summoned to write their memories, as Bartoli notes, "Clare would not have been absent."[231]

230 Leo remained a staunch defender of Francis's ideals after his friend's death and incurred great hardship as a result. He retreated to a hermitage, and hereafter we have only occasional glimpses of him. He appears to have passed his later years at the Porziuncola and spent much of that time writing various works about Francis. Leo remained very close to Clare throughout her life. He visited her frequently and was present, along with Angelo, when she died in 1253. Leo died at the Porziuncola, at an advanced age (his exact age is unknown), on November 15, 1271. He bequeathed to the order three notes written from the hand of Francis, one of which Leo carried on his person until his death. They remain the only extant autographs of Francis and are written in poor Latin. The mortal remains of brothers Leo, Masseo, Angelo, and Rufino are buried around Francis's tomb in the crypt of the Basilica of San Francesco. Leo is placed to Francis's right. (The remains of these four brothers were moved from the lower basilica to the area surrounding Francis's crypt in the 1930s.)

231 Bartoli, *Beyond the Legend,* 105.

CHAPTER 11

|||||||||||||||||||||||||||||||||||||||||

CLARITY

ven as Clare's physical presence was waning, her light would soon shine its brightest. As death began its creep over her in late summer 1253, two episodes defined the final act of her story, both of which crowned her life with perfect clarity. Both of them testify to the steadiness of her will and the tenderness of her heart.

Her Rule

The first episode involved the destiny of the "Form of Life," or Rule, that Clare wrote for her Order. The details of her Rule pertaining to day-to-day living were explored in Chapter Nine. Our concern here involves the overarching key elements that were the backbone of its writing. That includes the twofold intention of Francis regarding the ongoing attendance of the brothers in caring for the needs of the sisters and the uniquely Franciscan form of poverty. After Pope Innocent IV had imposed his own Rule on the Poor Sisters in 1247—a document Clare eschewed—she began the hard work of crafting hers, summoning early on the words and promise Francis conveyed to her directly:

> Because by divine inspiration you have made yourselves daughters and handmaids of the most High, most Exalted King, the heavenly Father, and have taken the Holy Spirit as your spouse, choosing to live according to the perfection of the holy Gospel, I resolve and

promise for myself and for my brothers always to have the same loving care and special solicitude for you as for them.[232]

And:

I, little brother Francis, wish to follow the life and poverty of our most high Lord Jesus Christ and of His most holy Mother and to persevere in this until the end; and I ask you, my ladies, and I give you my advice that you live always in this most holy life and poverty. And keep careful watch that you never depart from this by reason of the teaching or advice of anyone.[233]

The first reference highlights the vow he made that he and the brothers would always care for Clare and her sisters. The second refers to Francis's words of affirmation regarding the kind of poverty he embraced and was exhorting the women to appropriate. In her Rule, Clare summarizes her lifelong battle to uphold these two defining affirmations with the understated nuance that defined her words: "I, together with my sisters, have ever been solicitous to safeguard the holy poverty which we have promised the Lord God and blessed Francis."

Despite her solicitousness, her way of life and that of her sisters was under constant pressure from ecclesiastical powers that had resolved to keep the women's monasteries under the Benedictine paradigm. She fought this model because if women's communities enjoyed the benefit of dowries, this would at the same time relieve the friars of the need to render watch-care over the women, ostensibly nullifying Francis's proscribed seminal components.

We've already noted how Clare's battle was being waged even from the early days before Francis's death when, in 1218–19 (while Francis was in Egypt), Pope Honorius IV changed the terms of the existence of the women's monasteries, pressuring them to conform to the more

232 *CA:ED*, 118.
233 *CA:ED*, 118.

secure model of enclosure and financial security. To console Clare (and Francis), the Guardian of the Order, Bishop Ugolino (later Pope Gregory IX), allowed an exemption in the form of the "Privilege of Poverty" for the Poor Sisters at San Damiano. This privilege gave Clare her wish to engage somewhat autonomously with regard to both Franciscan poverty and reliance upon the brothers for sustenance. When Ugolino ascended to the papal throne in 1227 shortly after Francis's death, he pressed on with his larger goal of consolidating and unifying the women's houses under the Benedictine paradigm, while nevertheless renewing in 1228 the "Privilege of Poverty" exemption to accommodate Clare's wishes. Gregory died in 1241 and Innocent IV succeeded him.[234] He continued Gregory's campaign of consolidation, though he did not nullify Gregory's exemption for the Poor Sisters at San Damiano. Even so, in keeping with the larger plan, he crafted a Rule for all monasteries of the Poor Sisters, reinforcing the Benedictine model and further antagonizing Clare.

At this point she resolved to write her own Rule which she intended to submit to the pope for approval. It was the same document in which she summoned the words and promises of Francis himself, who by this point had been canonized and was deemed a saint.

Clare was older and growing weary of old battles. She was also proving to be stubbornly unyielding in her resolve to stay true to Francis's intention. Who could blame her? Whether inspired by pity, sentimentality, or simple resignation, some of Clare's ecclesiastical overseers began showing her sympathy. This is especially true of the Cardinal Protector of her Order, Cardinal Rainaldo di Ienne, in whom Clare confided much during these later years. After completing the document in 1252, she presented it to Cardinal Rainaldo for his approval, which he granted in September of the same year, approximately a year before Clare died. Thus, only one hurdle remained for Clare's battle to be won: the seal of approval by the Holy Father.

234 Innocent IV followed the very brief papacy of Celestine IV, whose tenure as pope lasted only a few months.

Clare was an excellent writer—lucid, spare, concise, grace-filled. Her "Form of Life" expressed a vision for the Poor Sisters that would have been unrecognizable to her at the time when she slipped away from her family home to join Francis to enter the religious life. She would not have envisioned the cloister. She would not have pictured that the rhythm of her days, day in and day out, would be marked by prayer, singing, and sewing, and that they would be constrained by immobility and her confinement to bed. Mendicant Franciscans were being martyred in foreign lands for their testimony and she longed to be among them! Those longings were overthrown in deference to another type of martyrdom: that of a long and confined life.

The vows she took when she embraced the Franciscan life included poverty, chastity, and obedience. The pivot point of Clare's religious life was the latter vow—obedience—more so even than the others. She exhorted her protege Agnes of Prague, as she faced battles, to ignore and even dismiss the pope's devices, as Clare had done consistently though respectfully. And while such advice could be seen as an act of disobedience and thus, an abdication of her vow, it paints a clear picture of the nature of Clare's true obedience. Clare's summons to Agnes to defy the pope and her own defiance of him were grounded in her understanding of her singular vocation and in service to her greater vow: the promise she made to Francis that—though heaven and earth be moved—she would be true to his mission. She would stay true if she died trying, and at points this seemed her destiny. Her singular obedience was to Francis, even when it violated her preference, as was the case when Francis insisted that she accept the role of abbess of her monastery. Such was the exercise of her vocation from which she did not waver, even when popes intervened and deemed her stubborn, if not delusional.[235]

But the tide was turning and Cardinal Protector Rainaldo, with the knowledge and consent of Pope Innocent IV, approved Clare's Rule. And

---

235 The single exception to Clare's unstinting obedience to Francis was in her keeping a cat. Francis, for all his love of animals, did not allow them in the brothers' and sisters' living quarters. Clare ignored this and found great comfort in her cat. Her love of felines has earned her the status of the Patron Saint of Cats.

the tightened screws loosened. She now awaited the definitive outcome of her quest in the form of the final authoritative imprimatur of the pope on her Rule, even as her strength was failing and her life waning.

The Dream

A second episode stands out in the final year of Clare's life,[236] and came in the form of a dream she had, the existence of which was disclosed only after her death. It was a telling dream and one that brought Clare great consolation, even as the world about her was growing dim.

During the investigation in the *Process of Canonization,* one of Clare's sisters—Sister Philippa, daughter of Lord Leonardo di Ghislerio and a childhood friend who entered the Order four years after Clare—recounted for the investigators this dream—which Clare had conveyed to her in detail—and which Clare also shared with several of her sisters:

Lady Clare also related how once, in a vision, it seemed to her she brought a bowl of hot water to Saint Francis along with a towel for drying his hands. She was climbing a very high stairway, but was going very quickly, almost as though she were going on level ground. When she reached Saint Francis, the saint bared his breast and said to the Lady Clare: "Come, take, and drink." After she had sucked from it, the saint admonished her to imbibe once again. After she did so what she had tasted was so sweet and delightful she in no way could describe it. After she had imbibed, that nipple or opening of the breast from which the milk comes remained between the lips of blessed Clare. After she took what remained in her mouth in her hands, it seemed to her it was gold so clear and bright that everything was seen in it as in a mirror.

236 There is not scholarly consensus about the date of this dream since none of the sisters noted the date when they recounted it during the *Process.* However, it is widely thought to have occurred during Clare's latter days as death drew near.

Had this strange dream become widely known during her canonization process, Clare's life might not have garnered uniform consensus attesting to her purity, piety, and daughter-like devotion to Francis. The dream suggested something other than a father-daughter devotion, medieval trends in gender transference notwithstanding.[237] Sister Philippa was bound before heaven to speak what she knew to be true of Clare, and this odd and shocking dream was part of that witness. Four other sisters during the investigation also similarly attested to the veracity of Philippa's account, having heard Clare tell of this dream.[238]

So it had to be dealt with.

There is no getting around the sensual nature of this dream and the potential for scandal should knowledge of it be made public during the investigation for Clare's canonization. Many scholars have wrangled about what to make of it. Of particular note is the work of Gerard Pieter Freeman.[239] Proceeding under the proviso that "it would be an illusion to think we could fully enter the dream world of a thirteenth-century nun," he makes a vigorous case that this bizarre tale belongs in the realm of being a *vision* from God rather than a dream wrought from Clare's unresolved subconscious.[240]

His reasons are sound and plausible. He highlights the fact that, of the four components of the canonization examination (including Clare's life; Clare's conversion; her way of living at the monastery; and her miracles),

237 Gerald Pieter Freeman notes in his chapter "Clare of Assisi's Vision of Francis. On the Interpretation of a Remarkable Dream," in *Dreams as Divine Communication in Christianity: From Hermas to Aquinas*, B.J. Koet, ed. Leuven-Paris-Walpole, MA (2012), 225–54: "Thirteenth-century men and women understood their sex differently from ours. They did not blush or giggle when speaking of themselves as a member of the opposite sex or when talking about a male breast giving milk."

238 The other sisters affirming the dream include: Sister Amata (fourth witness), *PC* 4:51–52; Sister Cecilia, *PC* 6:34–37; and Sister Balvina, *PC* 7:19–21.

239 See note 244.

240 Freeman's distinguishes between a vision and a dream, "discriminating between dreams and vision is notoriously hard in classical medieval stories and scholars do not agree on the difference between them. . . . From point of origin, a vision is caused by divine intervention, while a dream has no supernatural cause." He makes the point that the sister who recounted this dream during the *Process* considered it to be the latter.

Philippa's description of the dream was rendered during the phase when Clare's miracles were being explored. Moreover, her testimony about the dream was given in the context of her telling of two other dreams or visions associated with Clare's life. The first was a prophetic word Clare's mother received while in prayer during her pregnancy with Clare: she would "give birth to a light that will shine brilliantly in the world." Philippa then, secondly, told of the dream about Clare suckling from Francis's breast. Finally, she reiterated a vision Clare experienced on Christmas Eve in the last year of her life. A Christmas Mass was being celebrated at the Basilica of Saint Francis and she was unable to attend because of illness. Nevertheless she "saw" and heard it in all its vividness even as she rested alone in her bed at San Damiano. Freeman asserts the dream of Clare suckling from Francis's breast, positioned between the two other visions, "must be seen as a vision in the sense that [the sisters] perceived Clare's story as divine revelation." In this regard it must be interpreted as a whole without any isolating parts, though each part carries a specific meaning in the overall vision.

He divides the dream into three main "acts" or "scenes." In the first, he says, "Clare ascends the stairway and comes to St. Francis. The climbing is easy"; in the second, "Francis nurses Clare. The milk is delightful"; in the third, "Clare uses the nipple as a mirror. It is bright as gold." Within these scenes a variety of images are employed which serve as symbolic props. These include the hot water, the towel, the stairway, the male breast, breastfeeding, the mirror, and gold.

Henceforth, in Freeman's analysis, the various elements of the dream carry a wider theological significance in keeping with the rubric of its being a vision. For example, the image of the water and the towel, he suggests, is reminiscent of Jesus washing the feet of his disciples on the occasion of the Last Supper. He further cites the fact that Clare regularly washed the feet of her sisters and that foot-washing is a symbol of humility. Therefore, the hot water and towel, he says, bespeak Clare's humility. He concedes the point that in the dream Francis's *hands* and not his feet are washed and reckons with that discrepancy by suggesting that a woman washing a man's feet, in medieval thinking, would have been deemed too intimate. He similarly likens the image of the stairway as the pathway for growing in the virtue of humility, citing a chapter in Benedict's Rule that likens the image of a ladder to twelve steps toward humility.[241] He explores the common practice in the medieval mind of gender inversion to account for the otherwise steamy, sexual overtones of Clare suckling Francis's breast and his bidding her to do so a second time. At every point in the dream Freeman mounts a commendable defense as to how the dream could be, and ought to be, understood as symbolic vision and bereft of sexual overtones.

In the end he poses the most important question about the episode: Why would Philippa think this information would advance the cause of Clare's canonization?

The short answer is, it didn't.

As Freeman concedes, "the men wrote it down and then chose to forget it." The testimonies were never intended to be made public, given the scarcity of documentation about her life.[242] (They were private depositions.) When the official summary of these statements was handed over to the Curia commending canonization, no mention of the dream was included in those summaries. When investigation was complete and the official proclamation of the new saint was firmly established in the form of a papal decree and an officially sanctioned *Life* (biography), Clare's dream about Francis was absent from the record.

Yet the dream carried enough force for Clare to recount it to multiple sisters. And the sisters deemed it significant enough to be included in the investigation of Clare's canonization. It left an impression, in other words—an impression that the ecclesiastical overseers opted to dismiss.

---

241 The ladder to humility is from Benedict's Rule, ch. 7.

242 It is a boon and a treasure to students of Clare that this remarkable document was found. The text of the *Acts of the Process of Canonization* was found in an Umbrian Italian version dated in the fifteenth century and it was only as recently as 1920 that Zefferino Lazzeri discovered and published it.

The End

In May 1253 Pope Innocent IV was in Assisi and visited Clare on her sickbed. He was one of a few popes who entered the cloister to visit the esteemed Franciscan sister. The fact that popes visited her at various points through her life is a testament both to the high regard with which they held her and the hidden power she held, though immobile and tucked away in her "fortress of poverty," as one writer put it.

Sister Philippa says in her testimony that Clare was gravely ill when Innocent visited her, though it is unclear which papal visit she meant, as he visited her in May and then again in August a few days before her death. It could be that, during the first of those two visits, Clare pleaded with the pope to approve her Rule, perhaps emboldened by Cardinal Rainaldo's backing or out of the kind of clarity that attends the soul of one who is approaching death. It is not known what transpired between them during these visits other than the testimony of Sister Philippa, who said, "Lord Pope Innocent came to visit her since she was seriously ill. She then told the sisters: 'My daughters, praise God, because heaven and earth are not enough for such a benefit I have received from God. Today I have received Him in the Blessed Sacrament and I have also seen His Vicar.'"[243]

Philippa also recounts some poignant moments during Clare's final days and hours. Clare began to mutter aloud, saying things that confused her sisters. When one of them asked her who she was speaking to, she answered, "I am speaking to my soul." Some of her words were spoken too softly for the sisters to recount. At another point, one sister directed another to commit to memory the words Clare spoke. Clare overheard this and replied, "You will only remember these things I now say as long as He Who made me say them permits you."

Sister Philippa describes the final hours of Clare's life: "She learned a brother had come with letters bearing the papal bull. She reverently took

243 *CA:ED*, 160. Also note a: "Innocent IV was in Assisi in April, May, and from June to October 6, 1253. In his *Vita Innocentii IV*, Niccolò da Clavi records two visits of the pope to the saint. See F. Pagnotti, "Niccolò da Clavi e la sua vita di Innocenzo IV," *Archivio della Società Romana di Storia Patria*, XXI [1898]: 4–120."

it even though she was very close to death and pressed that seal to her mouth in order to kiss it. On the following day, Lady Clare passed from this life to the Lord . . . to the clarity of eternal light."[244] So Pope Innocent IV made it official; Clare got her Rule. The bull *Solet Annuere* was handed down on August 9, 1253, and Clare died within a day and a half. The bull confirmed the definitive Rule of Saint Clare, granting her and the sisters at San Damiano all privileges of poverty she had fought for. This made Clare the first woman in the history of Christendom to have been granted her own rule, putting her in the company of saints Augustine, Ignatius, Benedict, Dominic, and, of course, Francis.[245]

She was surrounded by her sisters in the final days and hours of her life. Her blood sister Agnes had returned from her monastery in Monticelli to be by Clare's side, and her beloved friends, Brothers Leo and Angelo, were also present. Sister Benvenuta described a vision that she saw:

> A multitude of virgins dressed in white, with golden crowns, silently entered the room through the half-closed door and took up the whole room. The brightness was such that every corner of the house was inundated with it. One of the most beautiful of all, wearing a crown greater and brighter than any of the others, came forward. She went to the bed and there she stretched over Clare a veil so thin that it covered her without hiding her. Then she bent down and put her face near that of the dying woman. And with that the vision disappeared and the room was again in shadow.[246]

Clare's last known words, on August 11, 1253, were uttered most of all to herself: "Go securely and in peace, my blessed soul. . . . And you, Lord, are blessed because You have created me."[247]

244 *CA:ED*, 162.
245 Her rule pertained only to San Damiano and not to other convents. After Clare died it disappeared. In the early 1900s the abbess at Santa Chiara found it hidden inside an old habit of Clare's, thus animating new hope that more documents may yet be found.
246 This is Arnoldo Fortini's translation of the vision described by the Eleventh Witness, Sister Benvenuto, *Life*, 365. See *CA:ED*, 182.
247 *LCl*; *CA:ED*, 46.

So she died as she lived, with a singular clarity about the hidden glory she perceived as through a mirror. She saw it behind the mirror she wrote about to Agnes of Prague, through which she beheld a bride festooned with jewels and "covered and arrayed in needlework and adorned with the flowers and garments of all the virtues as is becoming of the daughter and dearest bride of the Most High King." She saw it in the mirror she perceived in the vision of Francis, leaning on his breast and receiving his nourishment and consolation: "It seemed to her it was gold so clear and bright that everything was seen in it as in a mirror." And now, in these final moments, at long last she stepped through the mirror into the world which she had seen only in glimmers and dreams. Angelic virgins took her there, where Francis awaited her. And she saw, most pointedly, the one she had become and who in fact she had always been, the one God had always seen even in her most desolate sorrows. There is a light that only shines when all other lights go out. She could finally see it; she embodied it and understood. "Lord," she said, "You are blessed. You created *me*."

CHAPTER 12

||||||||||||||||||||||||||||||||||||||||||

CONCLUSION

I posed a question in the introduction of this book: Why would someone want to read about Clare of Assisi?

I am hard-pressed to measure Clare's significance in practical results. Yes, she exchanged a life of privilege for a radical embrace of penitence. Yes, she held her ground of conviction against insuperable odds. Yes, she defied popes. Yes, at long last, she won approval for her self-authored Rule. She kissed the papal seal affixed to it with her dying breath.

But so what? Seracchioli called Innocent IV's approval of her Rule simply "a caress of the Pope." She meant that the pope never intended his validation to carry any lasting significance in the trajectory of the Order. It was simply a gesture of affection to console the dying Clare who had dedicated her life to that singular purpose. Within a matter of a few years after Clare's death, the Poor Sisters (who came to be known as "the Poor Clares") were moved out of San Damiano inside the walls of Assisi. And a decade after her death, the Order lived under a new Rule. As was the case with Francis, so it was with Clare: after she died, everything changed.

Pope Innocent IV approved Clare's Rule on August 9, 1253, and she died on August 11. By October the pope had initiated the investigation for her canonization, including interviews with the Sisters and other people who knew Clare. This process continued into November. The pope died in 1254, and it was left to his successor, Pope Alexander IV, to finish the *process*. Alexander canonized Clare in 1255 and the official

Legend of her life was composed. At this point in the textual history of documents relating to Francis and Clare, they began to be written out of each other's stories. Bartoli points out that Francis appears only sparingly in Clare's *Legend*,[248] and in 1260, when Bonaventure completed the new "official" biography of Francis, *The Major Life*, Clare appears equally sparingly.[249] Thankfully, this lacuna in the "official" record is more than overcome in the testimonies taken during the *Process of Investigation for Canonization*, in which Francis's bond with Clare stands out as a defining theme of both their lives and is woven through every testimony.

In 1260 Clare's body was transferred to the newly built basilica inside the walls of Assisi. In 1261 Pope Alexander IV died and his successor, Pope Urban IV, wrote yet another new Rule for the Poor Clares. This is because, over the latter decades of Clare's life, as she fought her battles and popes made their concessions (such as the "Privilege of Poverty" exemption), and as various Forms of Life were fashioned, conferred, objected to, revised, and at long last dismissed in deference to Clare's hard-won Rule, the Order of the Poor Clares kept growing. And since Innocent IV's approval of Clare's rule pertained only to the convent at San Damiano, there had to be a single governing document that unified them all. That is why Urban IV wrote a new Rule in 1263.[250]

He changed the name to the "Order of Saint Clare" and recalibrated its mission along the lines previously drawn by Gregory IX, which Clare

248 Bartoli, *Saint Clare: Beyond the Legend*, 99.
249 Bonaventure, who had been elected Minister General of the Franciscan Order in 1257, had been given the task of writing the "official" biography of Saint Francis and set about a meticulous reordering and consolidating of the decisions and records of all previous ministers general, the result being the "definitive" biography of Francis called *The Major Life*. This version smoothed inconsistencies in earlier legends and highlighted Francis's life only with episodes that emphasized his sanctity. It was officially approved in 1263 and three years later, in an unprecedented action, the general chapter of Paris (a gathering of representatives from the Franciscan Order worldwide) ordered all previous legends of Francis destroyed in deference to Bonaventure's. Fortunately for historians and lovers of Francis and Clare, not all obeyed the decree.
250 It was also during this period that Francis's history and legacy were similarly being reconfigured under the guidance of then-Minister General Bonaventure. The "official" histories" of both Francis and Clare were each being drawn at this time and the role of each in the other's story was being diminished.

had decisively rebuffed. The new Rule incorporated some elements of Clare's Rule (such as the role of the abbess) yet did not at any point make direct reference to Clare's document.

Furthermore, though Clare always insisted (and verified in her Rule) that the mandate of her Order arose from Francis, nowhere in Urban's Rule is Francis referenced as the Order's founder. Worse, there is no reference to living the Gospel of Jesus as being the heart of Clare's vocation of poverty, which was the singular factor defining the mission of both Francis and Clare. Ultimately, Urban's Rule solidified the inevitable shift that Clare saw coming and that she fought against all her life. The Order was no longer rooted in the vision of Francis as grounded in the gospel. It was now an ecclesiastical entity, ordered around the dictates and sensibilities of Gregory IX, with only little bits of Clare's raw ideals sprinkled in here and there.[251]

So was all of Clare's striving for naught? What difference, in the end, did her hard-fought battles make? Why would Innocent IV affirm a Rule in 1253 he knew would eventually be overthrown knowing, in fact, that overthrowing it had always been part of the long-term plan? Were the popes mocking her?

Clare and Francis were wrestling with the true, literal application of the life and teaching of Jesus regarding what it meant to follow him in real life. They did not equivocate or reduce his teaching to abstract principles. They did what Jesus said was necessary in order to be his disciples. Their embrace of a life of poverty—whether they realized it or not—called back

---

251 Bartoli points out that, though, at the time, the majority of monasteries adopted the "Constitutions of Ugolino" (Pope Gregory IX) there remained a small contingent of monasteries that stayed true to the Rule of Saint Clare. Throughout the centuries, when there would arise reform movements among the Franciscans, the sisters frequently would seek to return to the Rule of Clare. Bartoli further notes that "in the second half of the twentieth century, when the Vatican Council invited all religious to recover the charism of their founders. . . . [T]he large majority of Clares felt free to choose to return to the Rule of Saint Clare," *Beyond the Legend*, 124. I spoke with a contemporary Third Order (female) Franciscan living in Assisi who works with the Poor Clares there and she told me that, today, the Sisters themselves own the property where they live (the Basilica and convent in Assisi) and that a few friars live in separate quarters to minister to their spiritual needs.

something that had been lost almost to the point of extinction in the Church, at least on the Italian peninsula. They were resetting the plumb line for what it meant to be "of Jesus." The plumb line had to be reset, as the institutional memory of the first-century Jesus had been grossly distorted, if not lost altogether. Maybe Francis and Clare did not see their vocation in these sweeping terms, but institutional reckoning was part of the meaning of their short vaulting lives. Clare, if she did nothing else, was determined to hold that plumb line. Her concern was to maintain and verify in a Rule what Francis had commissioned her to do and the way of life she was determined to uphold after his death. This was the singular purpose that defined all her days.

Even so, near the end of his life, Francis was essentially expelled from his own order because, as it grew and evolved, some maintained that his "gospel" dictates were too onerous. From the beginning, institutional pushback was working its will as these humble penitents attempted to live out their mission. The popes were left to deal with the ensuing chaos among the multitudes who followed them. I shared correspondence with Franciscan scholar Gerard Pieter Freeman years ago, and he put it this way: "Try to trust . . . Pope Gregory IX. He was trying to give women religious a legitimate place in the Church and going against the grain of many male religious [Orders]. He approved the poverty of the first Poor Clares but changed his views . . . probably because he saw poverty was too heavy for them. . . . I am almost the only one who has a good word for Ugolino [Gregory], but just try . . . to give him a chance."[252]

So it could be argued that the popes were not mocking Clare. They were navigating as best they could an intractable situation brought on by Francis and Clare. Regardless, the end result meant that despite their striving and best efforts, neither Francis nor Clare won the day for their cause.

But this is where we must remember Clare's theology and her realm of the mirror. Clare lived her life as if through the mirror, where the image looking back did not resemble the one gazing into it. Her earthly

252 Written correspondence we shared in late 2006 and early 2007.

visage was drawn and pale, often with wet eyes, while in the mirror she beheld a face of glory. When you live with that purview, "winning the day" belongs to the domain of the other side of the mirror. It could be thought of another way, as expressed in the Book of Hebrews: "Jesus died outside the gate. . . . Let us go to him outside the camp, bearing the insult he bore. For here we have no lasting city."[253] Clare, following Francis, went outside the gate to join her beloved Spouse there, to bear the shame he bore. Francis, too, joined him there. Once the line between that which was "inside" the camp and "outside" had been crossed, the portal into the everlasting city had been opened. By going with Jesus outside the camp, by means of embracing poverty—though the eyes of the world could see only rejection, scorn, sorrow, and impoverishment—Clare saw glory. That is why Francis wrote that poverty, "having been brought to us by Jesus Christ, shone more brightly than the sun and therefore the eyes of the flesh cannot see it or function in its light."[254]

"Winning the day" was never the point. In fact, you could say that Francis "lost" in the end. And Clare did too. But you could also say that *that* is the way of the Christian. Christians often lose. That is because they do not live to win; they live to give up their lives. The devil will happily devour a life that gives itself in such devotion. He will rob a Christian of everything and think he has stolen the victory, even as he thought he had stolen it from Jesus. But the devil is a fool and the prince of fools. The devil will never understand that, for the Christian, and especially for the Franciscan, the measure of a life is not about what has been accomplished. Nor is it even about what has failed. The measure of a life, in the Franciscan way, is found in what has been given up and transferred to a differing account. Union with Christ is to abide outside the gate. Or, to go back to Clare's imagery, union with Christ was found in the world on the other side of the mirror. While this other world is a world many of us long for and seek, it is the world the earliest Franciscans *inhabited*, on

253 Hebrews 13:12.
254 Fortini/Moak, 659, n. 92.

earth, as they lived out their days in poverty. Often in turmoil, weakness, illness, sorrow, and defeat, yes, Clare and Francis lost.

It's okay. They did not operate by the rules of the prince of this world— the prince of fools—just as Jesus did not operate by those rules. Jesus lost too. Christians tend to lose. Losing is the way in, the pivot point, the place where the supports and apparatus of the world collapse in a glorious exchange that unleashes invisible forces of an unconquerable world.

Finding the way into that kind of hope and accessing that kind of power is why anyone should want to read a book about Clare. It is also why, in the end, I wanted to write this book about her. There have been times in my life when I have felt outside the gate and couldn't see the glory in it. If there was glory to be seen there, I was blind to it. So I thought that if there was anyone who could lead the way to see the glory of living outside the camp, it would be one who spoke the words with her dying breath that God himself was blessed for having made her after a life of loss, sorrow, and struggle. I wanted to hear more from that person. There was something I could learn there.

Not many of us reach the place in our spiritual journeys where our testimony is mostly about the singular glory that God imparted to himself by creating us. We are not often given to understand that it is our mission to give back to God this unique glory and to bless *him* by it. Generally speaking, spiritual journeys involve a picture of divine actions moving earthward from heaven, coming down so as to find a place to land to bring new hope in the landscape of human sorrow. Clare's spiritual vision, at its pinnacle, went in the opposite direction.

Clare's testimony arose from earth to reach heaven until she saw herself as she was meant to be seen, taking her unique place in God's saving activity. "Glorify yourself" was the prayer Jesus prayed on the last night of his life. Imagine a human being so emptied of himself and so otherwise filled with beatitude that one's prayer is to realize the blessedness of one's own singular life as it is known to and seen by God, and then to give thanks for the marvelous gift of rendering back to God a life that blesses him. This is a uniquely Christian paradigm. And Clare, of all possible messengers, carried it to perfection. She embodied Christian truth—not dogmatically, but mystically and poetically, as one who inch by inch was stripped of all self-importance and earthly contrivances until there was nothing left except the skin and bone of her life lived out on an uncomfortable bed. That was it. That was the place of perfection where God's light found its fullest effulgence.

How much her unique pilgrimage had to do with the image of a bejeweled bride adorned with braids and tapestries is something that can be known only in the secrets shared between Clare and her heavenly Spouse. It doesn't matter in the end if she found her way to this place of beatitude by means of a mirror. She found it the best and only way she alone could find and claim it. She stayed her course. And her course, it could be said, completed her. Her course and your course and my course are not the same.

Clare would invite us all to find our place in God's orchestra, our course, and then do what we've been called to do with fleetness, prudent happiness, and singleness of purpose. She would remind us (as she reminded Agnes of Prague) always to "remember our beginnings," by which she would mean that singular moment of quickening or awakening or shattering when we understand that we belong to God alone. Only God has a claim on us. And with these tools in our sacks, on we go, as on she went, day by day, even minute by minute, doing the small things God placed before her that, over the course of a lifetime, configured a destiny. And if our eyes are fixed aright and our hearts ever being tuned toward heaven, we too will find that holy place, inside the mirror or outside the camp, where we finally understand the reason we were made and, more than that, the gift that we alone can render to God and his plan. We will see ourselves as with new clarity—*novum videre nos ipsi in claritate*. The operative word there is *claritate*, from which is derived the name Clare, whose subtle, sweeping, shattering light is showing us the way.

ACKNOWLEDGMENTS

I am grateful to many for their various efforts in support of my work on this project. My friends and colleagues in Assisi, as always, have proven invaluable. In particular I am indebted to Fra Carlo Bottero, Director of the Biblioteca del Sacro Convento, for his generosity of time and giving me space in the library to work. I especially appreciate, whenever I'm there, the special tours he gives me in the manuscript room where I see the handwritten words in medieval volumes that were penned by Francis's first followers. These special moments always elevate and inspire my work. I am similarly indebted to the historian and pilgrimage leader Angela Seracchioli, who drove me to special spots related to Clare's early years and also served as a translator when the need arose. My friend from many years back, and historian and tour guide extraordinaire, Simona Fanelli, has my heartfelt gratitude for making time to sit at my table and talk at length about Clare and her world, despite the demands of her busy schedule. I want also to thank the outstanding scholar and historian, Fra Pietro Maranesi, OFM. CAP., for his time and enthusiasm, meeting with me in an animated discussion that lent much insight into Clare's understanding of her religious life. I would be remiss not to offer special thanks to Dee Smith, an American Third Order Franciscan staying in Assisi with the Poor Clares. She helped me navigate the cloister to meet with one of the sisters and was always feeding me answers to my seemingly unending stream of questions, even from afar after I returned to the States. Beyond my friends in Italy, back home I owe a special debt of thanks to my gifted friends and colleagues Douglas LeBlanc and Kerry Pound, M.D., who read the early version of the manuscript and rendered valuable and wise feedback. I want to acknowledge the McConnell family—Eliza, Chip, Win and Nick—who graciously supported my work. And then there is Clare who, in her elusive and solicitous way, nudged and helped me throughout the writing, though few will believe it.

APPENDIX A

MAPS

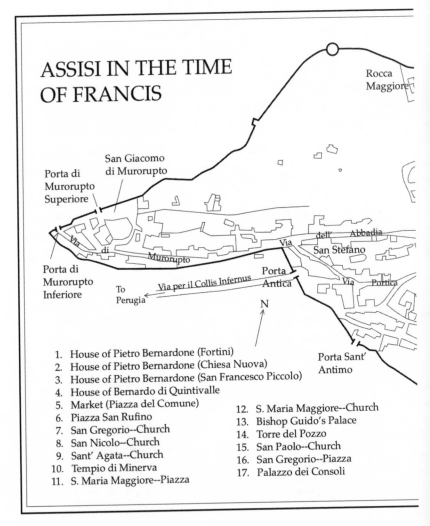

ASSISI IN THE TIME OF FRANCIS

Rocca Maggiore

San Giacomo di Murorupto

Porta di Murorupto Superiore

Porta di Murorupto Inferiore

Via di Murorupto

Via dell' Abbadia

San Stefano

Porta Antica

Via per il Collis Infernus

To Perugia

Via Portica

N

Porta Sant' Antimo

1. House of Pietro Bernardone (Fortini)
2. House of Pietro Bernardone (Chiesa Nuova)
3. House of Pietro Bernardone (San Francesco Piccolo)
4. House of Bernardo di Quintivalle
5. Market (Piazza del Comune)
6. Piazza San Rufino
7. San Gregorio--Church
8. San Nicolo--Church
9. Sant' Agata--Church
10. Tempio di Minerva
11. S. Maria Maggiore--Piazza
12. S. Maria Maggiore--Church
13. Bishop Guido's Palace
14. Torre del Pozzo
15. San Paolo--Church
16. San Gregorio--Piazza
17. Palazzo dei Consoli

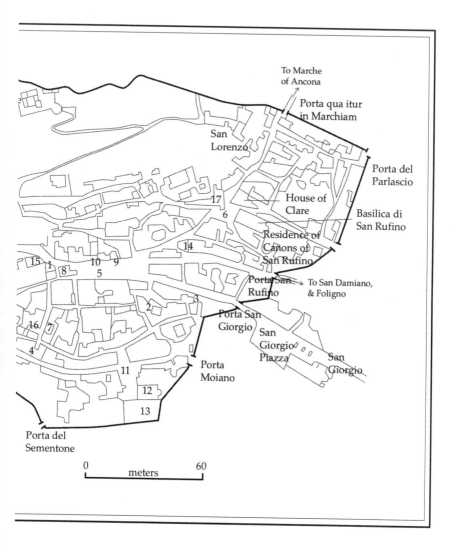

To Marche
of Ancona

Porta qua itur
in Marchiam

San
Lorenzo

Porta del
Parlascio

17

House of
Clare

6

Basilica di
San Rufino

14

Residence of
Canons of
San Rufino

15 1

10   9

8

5

Porta San
Rufino

To San Damiano,
& Foligno

2

3

Porta San
Giorgio

San
Giorgio
Piazza

San
Giorgio

16   7

Porta
Moiano

4

11

12

13

Porta del
Sementone

0   60

meters

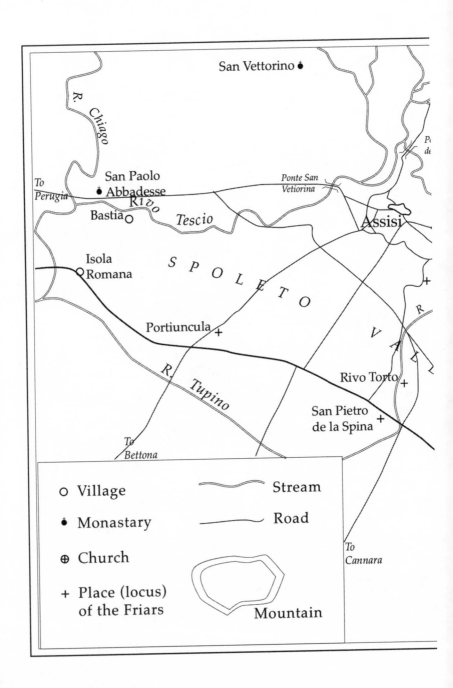

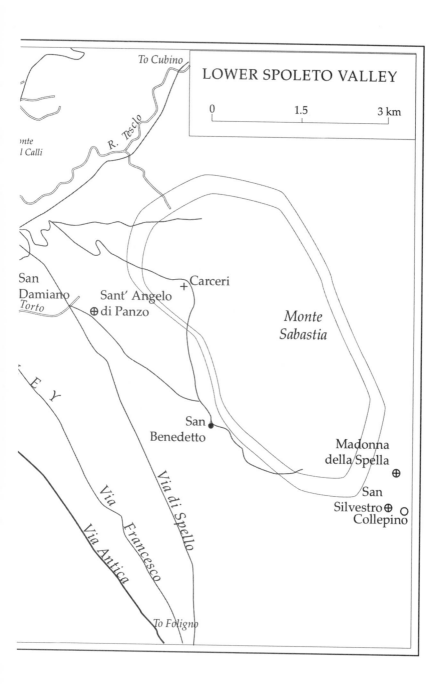

To Cubino

LOWER SPOLETO VALLEY

0   1.5   3 km

R. Tescio

*nte
l Calli*

San
Damiano
Torto

Sant' Angelo
⊕ di Panzo

+ Carceri

*Monte
Sabastia*

San
Benedetto

E Y

Madonna
della Spella
⊕

Via
Francesco

Via di Spello

Via Antica

San
Silvestro ⊕ ○
Collepino

To Foligno

SOURCE MATERIAL

CLARE'S LETTERS TO AGNES OF PRAGUE[255]

The First Letter to Agnes of Prague (1234)

To the esteemed and most holy virgin, Lady Agnes, daughter of the most excellent and illustrious King of Bohemia, Clare, an unworthy servant of Jesus Christ and useless handmaid of the enclosed Ladies of the Monastery of San Damiano, her subject and handmaid in all things, commends herself totally with special reverence that she may attain the glory of everlasting happiness.

I greatly rejoice and exult in the Lord on hearing the fame of Your holy conduct and irreproachable life, [a fame] that has wonderfully reached not only me but almost the whole world, and so not only I, but all who serve and desire to serve Jesus Christ are able to rejoice. For, though You, more than others, could have enjoyed the magnificence, honor, and dignity of the world and could have been married to the illustrious Emperor with splendor befitting You and His Excellency, You have rejected all these things and have chosen with Your whole heart and soul a life of holy poverty and bodily want. Thus You took a spouse of a more noble stock, Who will keep Your virginity ever unspotted and unsullied, the Lord Jesus Christ,

Whom in loving, You are chaste;
in touching, You become more pure;
in embracing, You are a virgin;
Whose strength is more robust, generosity more lofty,

255 *CA:ED*, 43–58.

Whose appearance is more handsome, love more courteous,

and every kindness more refined,

Whose embrace already holds you;

Who has adorned Your breast with precious stones, placed priceless pearls on Your ears, surrounded You completely with blossoms of springtime and sparkling gems

and placed on Your head a golden crown as a sign of Your holiness.

Therefore, most beloved sister, or should I say, Lady worthy of great respect, because You are the spouse and the mother and the sister of my Lord Jesus Christ and are beautifully adorned with the banners of an undefiled virginity and a most holy poverty, be strengthened in the holy service of the Poor Crucified undertaken with a passionate desire,

Who endured the suffering of the cross for us all,

delivering us from the power of the prince of darkness

to which we had been enslaved by the disobedience of our first parent,

thus reconciling us to God the Father.

O blessed poverty, who bestows eternal riches

on those who love and embrace her!

O holy poverty, God promises the kingdom of heaven and,

beyond any doubt, reveals eternal glory and

blessed life to those who have and desire her!

O God-centered poverty, whom the Lord Jesus Christ

Who ruled and still rules heaven and earth,

Who spoke and things were made,

came down to embrace before all else!

He says: For the foxes have dens, and the birds of the air have nests, but the Son of Man, Christ, has nowhere to lay His head, but bowing His head He gave up His spirit.

If so great and good a Lord, then, on coming into the Virgin's womb, wanted to appear despised, needy, and poor in this world, so that people who were very poor and needy, suffering excessive hunger of heavenly nourishment, may become rich in Him by possessing the kingdom of heaven, be very joyful and glad, filled with a remarkable happiness and a spiritual joy! Because, since contempt of the world has pleased You more than its honors, poverty more than earthly riches, You have sought to store up greater treasures not on earth but in heaven, where rust does not consume nor moth destroy nor thieves break in and steal, Your reward is very rich in heaven! And You are virtually worthy to be called a sister, spouse and mother of the Son of the Most High Father and of the glorious Virgin.

For I firmly believe that you know the kingdom of heaven is promised and given by the Lord only to the poor because she who loves what is temporal loses the fruit of love; that it is not possible to serve God and money, for either the one is loved and the other hated, or the one is served and the other despised; that one clothed cannot fight another naked, because she who has something to be caught hold of is more quickly thrown to the ground; that one who lives in the glory of earth cannot rule with Christ; and that it is easier for a camel to pass through the eye of a needle than for a rich person to enter the kingdom of heaven. Therefore, You have cast aside Your garments, that is, earthly riches, so that instead of being overcome by the one fighting against You, You will be able to enter the kingdom of heaven through the straight path and the narrow gate.

What a great and praiseworthy exchange: to receive the hundredfold in place of one, and to possess a blessed eternal life. Because of this I have led Your excellency and holiness, as best I can, to beg with humble prayers in the heart of Christ, that You be strengthened in His holy service, progressing from good to better, from virtue to virtue, so that He Whom You serve with the total desire of Your soul may bestow on You the reward for which You so long. Therefore, as much as I can, I also implore You in the Lord, to include me in Your most holy prayers, Your servant, though useless, and the other sisters with me in the monastery, who are all devoted to You. With the help [of Your prayers] we are able to merit the mercy of Jesus Christ, so that, equally together with You, we may merit to enjoy the everlasting vision. Farewell in the Lord and pray for me.

The Second Letter to Agnes of Prague (1235)

To the daughter of the King of kings, the servant of the Lord of lords, the most worthy spouse of Jesus Christ, and, therefore, the most noble Queen, Lady Agnes, Clare, the useless and unworthy handmaid of the Poor Ladies, greetings and may you always live in the highest poverty.

I give thanks to the Giver of grace from Whom, we believe, every good and perfect gift proceeds, because He has adorned you with such great titles of virtue and decorated you with signs of such perfection, that, since you have become such a loving imitator of the Father of all perfection, you might be made perfect and that there might be no imperfection in you for His eyes to see.

This is that perfection with which that King will join you to Himself in the heavenly bridal chamber where He is seated in glory on a starry throne, because you have despised the splendor of an earthly kingdom and considered of little value the offers of an imperial marriage. Instead, as someone zealous for the holiest poverty, in a spirit of great humility and the most ardent love, you have held fast to the footprints of Him to Whom you merited to be joined in marriage.

But since I know that you are filled with virtues, I will spare my words and not burden you with needless speech, even though nothing seems superfluous to you if you can draw from it some consolation. But because one thing is necessary, I bear witness to that one thing and encourage you, for love of Him to Whom you have offered yourself as a holy and pleasing sacrifice that you always be mindful of your commitment like another Rachel always seeing your beginning.

What you hold, may you hold,

What you do, may you do and not stop.

But with swift pace, light step, unswerving feet,

so that even your steps stir up no dust,

may you go forward

securely, joyfully, and swiftly,

on the path of prudent happiness,

believing nothing,

agreeing with nothing

that would dissuade you from this commitment

or would place a stumbling block for you on the way,

so that nothing prevents you from offering

your vows to the Most High in the perfection

to which the Spirit of the Lord has called you.

In all of this, follow the counsel of our venerable father, our Brother Elias, the Minister General, that you may walk more securely in the way of the commands of the Lord. Prize it beyond the advice of the others and cherish it as dearer to you than any gift. If anyone has said anything else to you or suggested any other thing to you that might hinder your perfection or that would seem contrary to your divine vocation, even though you must respect him, do not follow his counsel. But as a poor virgin embrace the poor Christ.

Look upon Him Who became contemptible for you, and follow Him, making yourself contemptible in this world for Him. Most noble Queen, gaze, consider, contemplate desiring to imitate Your Spouse, [Who] though more beautiful than the children of men became, for your salvation, the lowest of men, was despised, struck, scourged untold times throughout His entire body, and then died amid the suffering of the Cross.

If you suffer with Him, you will reign with Him.

Weeping with Him, you will rejoice with Him;

> dying on the cross of tribulation with Him,
> you will possess heavenly mansions with Him
> among the splendor of the saints
> and in the Book of Life your name will be called glorious among
> the peoples.

Because of this you shall share always and forever the glory of the kingdom of heaven in place of what is earthly and passing, and everlasting treasures instead of those that perish, and you shall live forever and ever.

Farewell, most dear Sister and Lady, because of the Lord, your Spouse; commend me and my sisters to the Lord in your fervent prayers, for we rejoice in the good things the Lord works in you through His grace. Remember us warmly to your sisters as well.

The Third Letter to Agnes of Prague (1238)

To the lady most respected in Christ and the sister to be loved before all mortals, Agnes, sister of the illustrious King of Bohemia, but now the sister and spouse of the Most High King of heaven, Clare, the most lowly and unworthy handmaid of Christ and servant of the Poor Ladies [wishes] the joys of redemption in the Author of salvation and whatever better thing can be desired.

I am filled with such joy at your well-being, happiness, and marvelous progress through which, I understand, you have advanced in the path you have undertaken to win a heavenly prize. And I sigh with so much more exultation in the Lord as I have known and believe that you supply most wonderfully what is lacking both in me and in the other sisters in following the footprints of the poor and humble Jesus Christ.

Truly I can rejoice, and no one can rob me of such joy, since, having at last what under heaven I have desired, I see that, helped by a special gift of wisdom from the mouth of God Himself and in an awe-inspiring and unexpected way, you have brought to ruin the subtleties of our crafty enemy, the pride that destroys human nature, and the vanity that infatuates human hearts; that by humility, the virtue of faith, and the arms of poverty, you have taken hold of that incomparable treasure hidden in the field of the world and of the human heart, with which you have purchased that by Whom all things have been made from nothing. And, to use the words of the Apostle himself in their proper sense, I judge you to be a co-worker of God Himself and a support for the weak members of His ineffable Body.

Who is there, then, who would not encourage me to rejoice over such marvelous joys? Therefore, dearly beloved, may you too always rejoice in the Lord. And may neither bitterness nor a cloud overwhelm you, O dearly beloved Lady in Christ, joy of the angels and crown of your sisters!

Place your mind before the mirror of eternity!
Place your soul in the brilliance of glory!
Place your heart in the figure of the divine substance
and, through contemplation,
transform your entire being into the image
of the Godhead Itself,
so that you too may feel what friends feel
in tasting the hidden sweetness that, from the beginning,
God Himself has reserved for His lovers.
And, after all who ensnare their blind lovers
in a deceitful and turbulent world
have been completely passed over,
may you totally love Him
Who gave Himself totally for your love,
At Whose beauty the sun and the moon marvel,
Whose rewards and their uniqueness and grandeur have no limits;
I am speaking of Him,
the Son of the Most High,
Whom the Virgin brought to birth
and remained a virgin after His birth.

May you cling to His most sweet mother who gave birth to a Son Whom the heavens could not contain, and yet she carried Him in the little cloister of her holy womb and held Him on her virginal lap. Who would not dread the treacheries of the enemy of humanity who, through the arrogance of momentary and deceptive glories, attempts to reduce to nothing that which is greater than heaven itself? Indeed, it is now clear that the soul of a faithful person, the most worthy of all creatures because of the grace of God, is greater than heaven itself, since the heavens and the rest of creation cannot contain their Creator; only a faithful soul is His dwelling place and throne, and this only through the charity that the wicked lack. The Truth says: Whoever loves me will be loved by My Father, and I too shall love him, and We shall come to him and make Our dwelling place with him. As the glorious virgin of virgins carried [Him] materially, so you, too, by following in her footprints, especially [those] of humility and poverty, can, without any doubt, always carry Him spiritually in your chaste and virginal body, holding Him by Whom you and all things are held together possessing that which, in comparison with the other transitory possessions of this world you will possess more securely. In this, certain worldly kings and queens are deceived, for, even though their pride may reach the skies and their heads touch the clouds, in the end they are as forgotten as a dung-heap!

Now concerning those matters that you have commissioned me to clarify for you, namely, what were the feasts that Your prudence should know, then, that except for the weak and the sick, for whom he advised and directed us to show every possible discretion in matters of food, none of us who are healthy and strong should eat anything other than Lenten fare, either on ferial days or on feast days. Thus, we must fast every day except Sundays and the Nativity of the Lord, on which days we may have two meals. And on ordinary Thursdays everyone may do as she wishes, so that she who does not wish to fast is not obliged. However, we who are well should fast every day except on Sundays and on Christmas.

During the whole of Easter, as the writing of Saint Francis tells us, and on the feasts of the Blessed Virgin Mary and of the holy Apostles, we are not obliged to fast, unless these feasts occur on a Friday. And, as I have already said, we who are well and strong always eat Lenten fare.

But our flesh is not bronze, nor is our strength that of stone, rather, we are frail and inclined to every bodily weakness! I beg you, therefore, dearly beloved, to refrain wisely and prudently from an indiscreet and impossible austerity in the fasting that you have undertaken. And I beg you in the Lord to praise the Lord by your very life, to offer the Lord your reasonable service and your sacrifice always seasoned with salt.

May you do well in the Lord, as I hope I do myself, and, in your holy prayers, remember me along with my sisters.

The Fourth Letter to Agnes of Prague (1253)

To her who is half of her soul and the special shrine of her heart's deepest love, to the illustrious Queen and Bride of the Lamb, the eternal King, to the Lady Agnes her most dear mother, and, of all the others, her favorite daughter, Clare, an unworthy servant of Christ and a useless handmaid of His handmaids in the monastery of San Damiano of Assisi: health and may she sing the new song with the other most holy virgins before the throne of God and the Lamb and follow the Lamb wherever He will go.

O mother and daughter, spouse of the King of all ages, if I have not written to you as often as both your soul and mine desire and long for, do not wonder at all or think that the fire of love for you glows with less delight in your mother's heart. No, this is the difficulty: the lack of messengers and the obvious dangers of the roads.

Now, however, as I write to your love, I rejoice and exult with you in the joy of the Spirit, O spouse of Christ, because, since you have totally abandoned the vanities of this world, like the other most holy virgin, Saint Agnes, you have been marvelously espoused to the spotless Lamb, Who takes away the sins of the world.

Happy, indeed, is she

to whom it is given to drink at this sacred banquet

so that she might cling with her whole heart to Him

Whose beauty all the blessed hosts of heaven

unceasingly admire,

Whose tenderness touches,

Whose contemplation refreshes, Whose kindness overflows,

Whose delight overwhelms,

Whose remembrance delightfully dawns,

Whose fragrance brings the dead to life again,

Whose glorious vision will bring happiness

to all the citizens of the heavenly Jerusalem,

which [vision], since He is the radiance of eternal glory

is the brightness of eternal light and

the mirror without blemish.

Gaze upon that mirror each day,

O Queen and Spouse of Jesus Christ,

and continually study your face in it,

that you may adorn yourself completely, within and without,

covered and arrayed in needlework and similarly adorned with the

flowers and garments of all the virtues, as is becoming, the daughter and

dearest bride of the Most High King.

Indeed, in that mirror, blessed poverty, holy humility,

and inexpressible charity shine forth as, with the grace of God,

you will be able to contemplate them throughout the entire mirror.

Look, I say, at the border of this mirror, that is, the poverty of Him

Who was placed in a manger and wrapped in swaddling clothes.

O marvelous humility! O astonishing poverty!

The King of angels, the Lord of heaven and earth, is laid in a manger!

Then reflect upon, at the surface of the mirror, the holy humility, at least

the blessed poverty, the untold labors and punishments that He endured

for the redemption of the whole human race.

Finally, contemplate, in the depth of this same mirror, the ineffable charity that He chose to suffer on the tree of the Cross and to die there the most shameful kind of death.

Therefore, that Mirror, suspended on the wood of the Cross, warned those passing by that here are things to be considered, saying: "All you who pass by the way, look and see if there is any suffering like my suffering!"

"Let us respond to Him," It says, "crying out and lamenting, in one voice, in one spirit: 'Remembering this over and over leaves my soul sinking within me!'"

O Queen of our heavenly King, may you, therefore, be inflamed ever more strongly with the fire of love! As you further contemplate His ineffable delights, riches and perpetual honors, and, sighing, may you cry out from the great desire and love of your heart: "Draw me after you, let us run in the fragrance of your perfumes, O heavenly Spouse! I will run and not tire, until You bring me into the wine-cellar, until Your left hand is under my head and Your right hand will embrace me happily, You will kiss me with the happiest kiss of Your mouth."

Resting in this contemplation, may you remember your poor little mother, knowing that I have inscribed the happy memory of you indelibly on the tablets of my heart, holding you dearer than all others.

What more? In your love may the tongue of the flesh be silent; may the tongue of the Spirit speak and say this: "O blessed daughter, because the love that I have for you can never be fully expressed by the tongue of the flesh," it says, "what I have written is inadequate. I beg you to receive my words with kindness and devotion, seeing in them at least the motherly affection that in the fire of charity I daily feel toward you and your daughters to whom I warmly commend myself and my daughters in Christ."

On their part, these daughters of mine, especially the most prudent virgin Agnes, our sister, recommend themselves in the Lord to you and your daughters as much as they can.

Farewell, my dearest daughter, with your daughters until we meet at the throne of the glory of the great God, and desire [this] for us. As much as I can, I recommend to your charity the bearers of this letter, our dearly beloved Brother Amatus, beloved of God and men, and Brother Bonaugura. Amen.

THE PAPAL DECREE OF CANONIZATION[256]

Alexander, Bishop, servant of the servants of God, to all our venerable brothers, the archbishops and bishops established throughout the kingdom of France: health and apostolic blessing.

Clare, brilliant by her bright merits,

by the brightness of her great glory in heaven,

and by the brilliance of her sublime miracles on earth,

shines brilliantly.

Clare, her strict and lofty way of religious life glows here on earth,

while the magnitude of her eternal rewards

radiates from above

and her virtue begins to dawn upon all mortal beings

with magnificent signs.

Clare: here [below] she was endowed with the privilege

of the most exalted poverty;

on high she is repaid by an inestimable source of treasure;

[Clare]: she is shown full devotion and immense honor by all.

Clare: her brilliant deeds distinguished her here [on earth].

Clare: while on high the fullness of the divine light shines on her.

Clare: her amazing works of wonder make her known to the Christian people.

O Clare, endowed with so many brilliant titles!

Bright even before your conversion,

brighter in your manner of living,

brighter still in your enclosed life,

and brilliant in splendor after the course of your mortal life!

256 *CA:ED*, 263–71.

In this Clare, a clear mirror of example has been given to this world;
by her, the sweet lily of virginity is offered among the heavenly delights;
by her, obvious remedies are felt here on earth.

O the inestimable brilliance of blessed Clare!
The more eagerly she is sought for something,
the more brilliant she is found in everything!
This woman, I say, was resplendent in the world,
shone brilliantly in her religious life;
enlightened as a radiant beam in her home,
dazzled as lightning in the enclosure.
She shone forth in life; she is radiant after death.
Enlightening on earth, she dazzles in heaven!

O how great is the vibrancy of this light
and how intense is the brilliance of its illumination!
While this light remained certainly in a hidden enclosure,
it emitted sparkling rays outside.
Placed in the confined area of the monastery,
yet she was spread throughout the wide world.
Hidden within, she extended herself abroad.
Yes, Clare hid, yet her life has come to light.
Clare was silent, yet her fame was proclaimed.
She was hidden in a cell, but was known in cities.

It should not be surprising that a light so enkindled,
so illuminating could not be kept hidden
without shining brilliantly and giving bright light in the house of the Lord;
nor could a vessel filled with perfume be concealed
so it would not give fragrance
and suffuse the Lord's house with a sweet fragrance.

Moreover, since with her harshness she broke the alabaster jar of her body
in the severity of her cloistered solitude,

the whole aura of the Church was thoroughly imbued
with the fragrance of her sanctity.

While still a young girl in the world, she was striving to pass rapidly
along a clean path, past the fragile and unclean world. Keeping the
precious treasure of her virginity with an undiminished modesty, she
carefully dedicated herself to works of kindness and brilliance, so that her
reputation spread freely to those near and far. After hearing this praise,
blessed Francis immediately began to encourage her and to lead her to
the perfect service of Christ.

Quickly adhering to the sacred admonitions of this man and desiring to
reject entirely the world with everything earthly and to serve the Lord
alone in voluntary poverty, she fulfilled this as quickly as she could. At
last she finally changed all her goods into alms and distributed them as
resources for the poor, so that, one with him, whatever she had she too
would consider for the service of Christ.

Then, fleeing from the clamor of the world, she went down to the church
in the field and, after receiving the sacred tonsure from blessed Francis
himself, she proceeded to another. When her relations endeavored to
bring her back, she immediately took hold of the altar and its cloths,
uncovered her shorn head and resisted her relatives strongly and firmly
in this way. She could not permit herself to be separated from God's
service because she was already joined to Him with her whole mind.

Finally, she was led by the same blessed Francis to the church of Saint
Damian outside of Assisi, from which she took her origin. There, for
the love and assiduous worship of His name, the Lord caused many
companions to flock to her. The distinguished and sacred Order of Saint
Damian, now widely diffused throughout the world, came and had its
salutary beginning from this woman.

This woman, encouraged by blessed Francis himself,

gave the beginning of following a new and holy observance.

This woman was the first and solid foundation

of this great religion.

This woman stood as the cornerstone of this lofty work.

This woman, noble by birth, but nobler by manner of life,

eminently preserved the virginity she had already protected

from the first under this rule of holiness.

Her mother, named Ortolana, intent upon pious deeds, followed her daughter's footprints and afterwards accepted this religious way of life. In this excellent garden which had produced such a plant for the Lord, she happily ended her days. But after a few years, that blessed Clare, very much urged by the insistence of the same Saint Francis, accepted the government of the monastery and the sisters.

This woman was undoubtedly a very lofty and outstanding tree

with far-reaching branches

that brought forth the sweet fruit of religion

in the meadow of the Church.

To its refreshing shade, under its delight,

many students of the faith ran and still run from everywhere

tasting fruit of every kind.

This woman was

a clear spring of the Spoleto Valley

that offered a new fountain of living water

for the refreshment and comfort of souls,

a fountain that has already irrigated the nursery of religion

through different rivulets in the precincts of the Church.

This woman was a lofty candelabra of sanctity,

shimmering brightly in the tabernacle of the Lord,

to whose remarkable splendor

many have and are still hastening,

lighting their lamps by its light.
This woman truly planted and cultivated
a vineyard of poverty in the field of the faith,
from which the abundant and rich fruits of salvation
have been gathered.
This woman established in the estate of the Church
a garden of humility
hedged in by need of a multiplicity of things
in which a great abundance of virtue flourishes.

This woman built in the area of religion
a citadel of strict abstinence
in which a vast abundance of spiritual food was administered.
This woman was the first of the poor, the leader
of the humble, the teacher of the continent, the abbess of the penitents.
This woman governed her monastery and within it the family
entrusted to her with solicitude and prudence, in the fear and service
of the Lord, and with the full observance of the Order:
vigilant in caring, assiduous in ministering,
attentive in exhorting, diligent in admonishing,
moderate in correcting, measured in commanding,
unwavering in compassion,
discerning in silence, mature in speech,
and experienced in everything pertaining to perfect government,
wanting to serve more than to command,
to honor than to be extolled.

Her life was an instruction and a lesson to others:
in this book of life;
some learned the rule of living,
in this mirror of life others learned to behold the paths of life.
To be sure, she remained in the body on earth,
yet she was dwelling in spirit in heaven:

a vessel of humility, an armoire of chastity,
the fire of love, the fragrance of benevolence, the vigor
of patience, the bond of peace, and the communion of familiarity;
Meek in word, gentle in deed,
and lovable and accepting in everything.

Because each one is stronger after overcoming an enemy, she had only the bare ground and sometimes twigs for her bed, and [a piece of] hard wood as pillow for her head in order to grow stronger in spirit after her body was repressed. Content with one tunic with a mantle of poor, discarded, and coarse material, she used these lowly clothes to cover her body. Near her flesh she wore a rough shirt made out of horsehair. Strict as well in food and disciplined in drink, she restrained herself so much by abstinence from these things that for a long time she did not taste any food three days a week, on Monday, Wednesday, and Friday. On the other days, when she limited herself to a meager bit of food, others marveled that she was able to survive on so rigorous a diet.

Moreover, she spent day and night especially giving herself assiduously to vigils and prayers. When she was finally laid up with long-term illness so she could not raise herself by physical exertion, she was lifted up with the help of the sisters. With supports for her back, she worked with her own hands, not to be idle even in her sickness. Then, out of the linen made by her skill and labor, she had many corporals made for the sacrifice of the altar and had them distributed throughout the plains and mountains of Assisi.

She was, above all, a lover and firm supporter of poverty. She so rooted it in her spirit, so fixed it in her desires, that, firmer in love of it and more ardent in its embrace, she never departed from her stronger and delightful union with it for any necessity. She could not be induced by any persuasion to consent to have any possessions in her monastery, even though Pope Gregory of happy memory, our predecessor, thinking about the great indigence of her monastery, generously wanted to endow sufficient and appropriate possessions for the sustenance of her sisters.

In truth, because a great and splendid light cannot be restrained from displaying the brilliance of its rays, the power of holiness shone in her life with many and various miracles. Thus she restored the voice of one of the sisters of the monastery [after] it had been almost totally lost for a long time. She restored the ability to speak to another who had long lost the use of her tongue. She opened the deaf ear of another. She cured by making the sign of the Cross over them: one struggling with a fever, one swollen with dropsy, one infected with a fistula, and others oppressed with various ailments. She healed a certain brother of the Order of Lesser Ones from insanity.

Once when, by accident, the oil in the monastery was totally depleted, she called for the brother assigned to gather alms for that monastery. She took a jar, washed it, and placed it empty by the door of the monastery so that the same brother would take it for acquiring oil. When he went to pick it up, he found it filled with oil, a gift of divine generosity.

Again, when one day only a half a loaf of bread was available for feeding the sisters in that monastery, she commanded that half [of it] be distributed in pieces among the sisters. He Who is the living bread and gives food to the hungry multiplied it in the hands of the one who broke it so that there were then fifty sufficient portions made and distributed to the sisters seated at table.

The preeminence of her merits was made known through these and other signs while still living. When she was about to die, a white-robed choir of blessed virgins crowned with glittering crowns, among which one seemed to be more eminent and brilliant, was seen to enter the house where that servant of Christ lay ill. She was seen to approach Clare's bed and, on her behalf, to show, as it were, the duty of visitation and comforting the sick with a certain human zeal.

After her death, however, a certain man suffering from epilepsy and unable to walk because of a withered leg, was brought to the tomb. There he was cured from both infirmities, his leg made a noise as if it were breaking. The hunchbacked and the paralyzed, the mad and demented received perfect health in that same place. Someone who had lost the use of his right hand by a violent blow so that it was totally useless had it completely restored to its original state through the merits of the saint. Another who had long lost the light of his eyes in blindness came to her tomb under the guidance of another. After he recovered his sight there, he returned home without a guide.

The venerable virgin shines with these and so many other glorious deeds and miracles. What her mother heard when she was pregnant with her and was praying appears to be clearly fulfilled: that she would give birth to a light that would illumine the entire world.

Therefore let Mother Church rejoice
that she had begotten and reared such a daughter
who as a parent fruitful with virtues
has produced many daughters of religion by her example,
and has trained them for the perfect service of Christ by her
thorough teaching.
Let the devout multitude of the faithful be glad
that the King and Lord of heaven
has chosen their sister and companion
as His spouse
and has introduced her with glory
to His lofty and brilliant palace.
Finally, let the multitude of saints rejoice
that the nuptials of a new royal bride are being celebrated
in their heavenly midst.

Therefore, because it is fitting the universal Church venerate on earth her whom the Lord exalted in heaven; because her sanctity of life and miracles are very evident from a thorough and careful investigation, a distinct examination, and a solemn discussion, even though, both near and far, her deeds were widely known before this. By the common advice and assent of our brothers and all the prelates who were then at the Holy See, and relying firmly upon the divine omnipotence, We, by the authority of the blessed Apostles, Peter and Paul, and our own, have directed she be inscribed in the catalogue of the holy virgins.

Therefore, We admonish and earnestly exhort all of you, commanding through the apostolic letters addressed to you, that you devoutly and solemnly celebrate the feast of this same virgin on the forty-second of the Ides of Augusta and that you have it venerably celebrated by your subjects, so you may merit to have a pious and diligent helper before God.

And so a multitude of people may come together more eagerly and in greater numbers to venerate her tomb, and so her feast day may be honored with greater numbers, to all who are truly contrite and have confessed their sins, and who humbly seeking her aid go each year with reverence to this tomb on the feast of this same virgin or during its octave, We, relying on the mercy of the All-Powerful God and on the authority of His Apostles, Peter and Paul, grant an indulgence of one year and forty days from the punishment due to their sins.

Given at Anagni, the sixth kalends of October, in the first year of our pontificate.

GLOSSARY OF TERMS

Abbot/Abbess: A friar or sister who is in charge of particular monastery.

Basilica/Cathedral: *Basilica* was originally used to describe a Roman public building; the term has evolved to refer to a large and important church that has been given special ceremonial rites by the pope while retaining an aspect of public accessibility for architectural, artistic, or ecclesiastical purposes. A *cathedral*, on the other hand, is a Christian church that contains the seat of a bishop. It is intended for worship and serves as the bishop's seat, thus as the central church of a diocese.

Bull (Papal bull): In Roman Catholicism, a papal bull is an official papal letter or document. The name is derived from the lead seal (*bulla*) traditionally affixed to such documents. Since the twelfth century it has designated a letter from the pope carrying a seal that shows the heads of the apostles Peter and Paul on one side and the pope's signature on the other.

Curia: The Roman Curia, taken from the Latin word that means "court," is the administrative counsel of the central governing body of the Roman Catholic Church. It is comprised of the pope and cardinals.

Divine Offices: Saint Benedict of Nursia (c. 480–543) is credited with creating a structure organization for the liturgy of offering prayers at various points of the day, including morning, at the third hour, the sixth, the ninth, the evening, and at "cock-crowing." The eight "Divine Hours," called the Divine Offices, are known by the following names:

MATINS (*during the night or pre-dawn hours of the morning*)

LAUDS (*at dawn*)

PRIME (*First Hour = 6 a.m.*)

TERCE (*Third Hour = 9 a.m.*)

SEXT (*Sixth Hour = 12 noon*)

NONE (*Ninth Hour = 3 p.m.*)

VESPERS ("*at the lighting of the lamps*"—*evening*)

COMPLINE (*before retiring*)

General Chapter: The gathering of all elected representatives of the order from all provinces to discuss business, make decisions, share fellowship, and set a course for the future.

Hagiography: An important literary genre in the early Christian church, providing historical information as well as inspirational stories and legends. (See below).

Indulgence: In early Roman Catholic theology it is the full or partial remission of temporal punishment due to sins granted forgiveness by the Church after the sinner has confessed and received absolution, or in some cases given money. Martin Luther's challenge of the abuse of indulgences ignited the sixteenth-century Reformation.

Legend: A book of record of the deeds of a saint; not intended to be a biography in the strict sense.

Mendicant (Latin *mendicare*, "to beg"): A member of a religious order in the Roman Catholic Church who takes a vow of poverty renouncing personal and communal property. The term has evolved to describe those in the penitential movement who went from place to place to preach.

Minister General: The head of the order within each respective branch (Conventual, Observant, Capuchin).

Order of Friars Minor:

Observant (OFM): The Observant branch strives to uphold the simple lifestyle modeled by Francis. They live in hermitages. Their tunics are brown. They shave.

Conventual (OFM CONV.): The Conventuals, in the Middle Ages, was a generic designation for Franciscans who lived in a stable house (*conventus* in Latin) and not in caves and hermitages. This branch encourages education and the building of universities. Their tunics are gray or black. They wear blue jeans outside the convent.

Capuchin (OFM CAP.): The Capuchin friars, which evolved in the sixteenth century, sought to return to and uphold the primitive way of life in solitude and penance as practiced by the founder of their order. They wear a brown tunic and usually have long beards.

Order of Saint Clare of Assisi or "Clares" (osc): The "Poor Clares," as they are also sometimes called, was a Franciscan Order founded by Clare (as the Order of Poor Ladies) to establish communities of women who wanted to embrace the penitential life as embraced by Francis.

Third Order Franciscans (tor): Also called the sfo—Secular Franciscan Order—was created in 1221 by Francis to accommodate brothers and sisters of the penitential movement who wished to live by the order's convictions but were prevented from joining because of marriage or other ties.

Penitent: In the twelfth and thirteenth centuries religious penitents were those who put themselves in the service of God by attaching themselves in service to a particular church or monastery. In all cases, the emphasis of the penance was to practice justice and mercy, to trust in God, to be of pure heart and intent, to have a zeal for Christ and the Scripture, and to be open to God's grace and inspiration. Most of the participants had little or no formal theological training and many developed heretical beliefs.

Rule: The governing document of a religious order.

Sacro Convento: The friary, or living quarters, in Assisi connected to the Basilica of San Francesco.

Saracens: Another name for the Arab empire (Muslim) under the rule of the Umayyad and Abbadis dynasties.

Templars: Also known as Knights Templars, they were a medieval Christian military order prominent in the Crusades from the early 1100s until the early 1300s.

Tonsure: In the Roman Catholic Church the "first tonsure" (a symbolic cutting of hair about the size of a coin leaving a bare spot toward the back of the head) was, in medieval times, the rite of qualifying someone for the civil benefits then enjoyed by clerics, primarily the privilege to preach.

*Renaissance artist Simone Martini's depiction of a member of the nobler class,
Jacopa dei Settisoli, which is wrongly marketed as the image of St. Clare.
(Lower Basilica of San Francesco in Assisi.)*

*Clare grieving the death of Francis in Giotto's fresco cycle in the
Upper Basilica of San Francesco in Assisi.*

RESOURCES (SELECTED)

Armstrong, Regis J., OFM CAP., *Clare of Assisi: Early Documents.* Hyde Park, NY: New City Press, 2006.

Armstrong, Regis J., OFM CAP., J. A. Wayne Hellmann, and William J. Short, eds. *Francis of Assisi: Early Documents.* 3 vols. Hyde Park, NY: New City Press, 1999.

Bartoli, Marco. *Clare of Assisi.* Trans. Frances Teresa. Quincy, IL: Franciscan Press, 1993.

Bartoli, Marco. *Saint Clare: Beyond the Legend.* Cincinnati, OH: Franciscan Media, 2010.

Chesterton, G. K. *Saint Francis of Assisi.* Garden City, NY: Doubleday/ Image Books, 1951.

Cunningham, Lawrence S. *Francis of Assisi: Performing the Gospel Life.* Grand Rapids, MI: Eerdmans, 2004.

Cuthbert, Father, OSFC. *The Romanticism of St. Francis.* New York: Longmans, Green & Co., 1915.

Dalarun, Jacques. *The Misadventure of Francis of Assisi: Toward a Historical Use of the Franciscan Legends.* Trans. Edward Hagman. Saint Bonaventure, NY: Franciscan Institute Publications, 2002.

De Robeck, Nesta. *St. Clare of Assisi.* Chicago: Franciscan Herald Press, 1980.

Eco, Umberto. *The Name of the Rose.* New York: Harcourt & Brace, 1983.

Englebert, Omer. *St. Francis of Assisi: A Biography.* Ann Arbor, MI: Servant Books, 1979.

Fonti Clariane. Perugia, IT: Edizione Porziuncola, Santa Maria degli Angeli, 2013.

Fortini, Arnaldo. *Francis of Assisi: A Translation of Nova Vita di San Francesco.* Trans. Helen Moak. New York: Crossroad, 1992.

Freeman, Gerald Pieter. "Clare of Assisi's Vision of Francis. On the Interpretation of a Remarkable Dream." *Dreams as Divine Communication in Christianity: From Hermas to Aquinas*, B.J. Koet, ed. Leuven-Paris-Walpole, MA (2012), 225–54.

Frugoni, Chiara. *Francis of Assisi: A Life.* New York: Continuum, 1998.

Frugoni, Chiara. *Una solitudine abitata: Chiara d'Assisi.* Roma: Laterza, 2006.

Green, Julien. *God's Fool: The Life and Times of Francis of Assisi.* Trans. Peter Heinegg. San Francisco: Harper & Row, 1985.

Habig, Marion A., ed. *St. Francis of Assisi: Writings and Early Biographies: English Omnibus of the Sources for the Life of St. Francis.* 2 vols. Trans. Raphael Brown, Benen Fahy, Placid Hermann, Paul Oligny, Nesta de Robeck, Leo Sherley-Price. Quincy, IL: Franciscan Press, 1991.

Jörgensen, Johannes. *Saint Francis of Assisi: A Biography.* Garden City, NY: Doubleday/Image, 1955.

Knox, Leslie S. *Creating Clare of Assisi, Female Franciscan Identities in Later Medieval Italy.* Leiden, The Netherlands: Brill, 2008.

Ledoux, Claire Marie. *Clare of Assisi.* Trans. Colette Joly Dees. Cincinnati: St. Anthony Messenger Press, 2003.

Magro, Pasquale M. *Guida completa all'iconografia della Basilica di San Francesco in Assisi.* Assisi, IT: Case Editrice Francescana, 1996.

Magro, Pasquale M. *Il simbolismo cristiano della chiesa-reliquiario di San Francesco in Assisi.* Assisi, IT: Casa Editrice Francescana, 1993.

Mueller, Joan. *The Privilege of Poverty.* University Park, PA: Pennsylvania State University Press, 2006.

Mueller, Joan. *Clare's Letters to Agnes, Texts and Sources.* St. Bonventure, NY: The Franciscan Institute, St. Bonaventure University, 2001.

Murray, Wendy. *A Mended and Broken Heart, the Life and Love of Francis of Assisi.* New York: Basic Books, 2008, 2012.

Nirit, Ben-Aryeh Debby. *The Cult of St. Clare of Assisi in Early Modern Italy.* Surrey, UK: Ashgate, Farnham, 2014.

Petroff, Elizabeth Alvilda. *Medieval Women's Visionary Literature*. New York, New York: Oxford University Press, 1986.

Sabatier, Paul. *Vie de saint François d'Assise* (Paris, 1894 and 1931). Italian trans. C. Ghidaglia and C. Pontani, *Vita di San Francesco d'Assisi* (Rome, 1926).

Sabatier, Paul. *The Road to Assisi: The Essential Biography of St. Francis.* Intro. and annotation Jon M. Sweeney. Brewster, MA: Paraclete Press, 2002.

Seraphin, Mary, PCPA. *Clare: Her Light and Her Song.* Chicago: Franciscan Herald Press, 1984.

Spoto, Donald. *Reluctant Saint: The Life of Francis of Assisi.* New York: Penguin, 2002.

Steegmann, Mary G., trans. *The Book of Divine Consolation of the Blessed Angela of Foligno.* Introduction by Algar Thorold. London: Chatto and Windus, 1909.

Journal Articles

Bigaroni, Marino. "San Damiano - Assisi: The First Church of Saint Francis. *Franciscan Studies,* Vol. 47 (1987), 45–97.

Fortini, Arnaldo. "New Information Concerning Clare of Assisi." *Greyfriars Review,* 7 (1993): 21–63.

Fortini, Gemma, and Finbarr Conroy. "The Noble Family of St. Clare of Assisi." *Franciscan Studies* Vol. 42 (1982), pp. 48-67.

Fortini, Gemma, and Finbarr Conroy. "The Contribution of Arnaldo Fortini to Franciscan Studies," trans. Finbarr Conroy. *Franciscan Studies,* vol. 43, annual 21. St. Bonaventure, NY: Franciscan Institute, St. Bonaventure University, 1983.

Johnson, Timothy, J. "Clare, Leo, and the Authors of the Fourth Letter to Agnes of Prague." *Franciscan Studies,* 62 (2004): 91-100.

Knox, Lezlie. "Audacious Nuns: Institutionalizing the Franciscan Order of Saint Clare." *Church History* 69:1 (March 2000): 41-62.

Micó, Julio, OFM CAP. "The Spirituality of St. Francis." *Greyfriars Review,* 7 (1993): 1–26.

Mooney, Catherine M. "The 'Lesser Sisters' in Jacques de Vitry's 1216 Letter." *Franciscan Studies,* Vol. 69 (2011): 1–29.

Padovese, Luigi. "Clare's Tonsure: Act of Consecration or Sign of Penance?" *Greyfriars Review,* 6 (1992): 67–80.

Robinson, Pascal. "St. Clare." *Franciscan Essays,* ed. Paul Sabatier, et al. Aberdeen, UK: University Press, 1912: 31–49.

Valerio, A. "Women in the 'Societas Christiana': 10th - 12th centuries." *Theology Digest,* 33:1 (Spring, 1986): 155–58.

INDEX

ABOUT THE AUTHOR

Award-winning author and journalist Wendy Murray has reported on and written about religion for over thirty years. She graduated with an M.A.T.S. in New Testament from Gordon-Conwell Theological Seminary and, for many years, served as an editor and Senior Writer at *Christianity Today* magazine. Her work has also appeared in *Books & Culture, The Christian Century, Publishers Weekly, Beliefnet.com*, and *Patheos.com*. She has written several books, including a biography of St. Francis of Assisi, *A Mended and Broken Heart* (Basic Books). She currently lives in the Boston area where she farms with two of her three grown sons.

Other Books by Wendy Murray (Selected)

A Mended and Broken Heart: The Life and Love of Francis of Assisi
Day of Reckoning: Columbine and the Search for America's Soul
Sacred Journeys
Facing Forward
On Broken Legs
The Warrior King

ABOUT PARACLETE PRESS

Who We Are

As the publishing arm of the Community of Jesus, Paraclete Press presents a full expression of Christian belief and practice—from Catholic to Evangelical, from Protestant to Orthodox, reflecting the ecumenical charism of the Community and its dedication to sacred music, the fine arts, and the written word. We publish books, recordings, sheet music, and video/DVDs that nourish the vibrant life of the church and its people.

What We Are Doing

BOOKS | PARACLETE PRESS BOOKS show the richness and depth of what it means to be Christian. While Benedictine spirituality is at the heart of who we are and all that we do, our books reflect the Christian experience across many cultures, time periods, and houses of worship.

We have many series, including *Paraclete Essentials; Paraclete Fiction; Paraclete Poetry; Paraclete Giants;* and for children and adults, *All God's Creatures*, books about animals and faith; and *San Damiano Books*, focusing on Franciscan spirituality. Others include *Voices from the Monastery* (men and women monastics writing about living a spiritual life today), *Active Prayer*, and new for young readers: *The Pope's Cat*. We also specialize in gift books for children on the occasions of Baptism and First Communion, as well as other important times in a child's life, and books that bring creativity and liveliness to any adult spiritual life.

The MOUNT TABOR BOOKS series focuses on the arts and literature as well as liturgical worship and spirituality; it was created in conjunction with the Mount Tabor Ecumenical Centre for Art and Spirituality in Barga, Italy.

MUSIC | PARACLETE PRESS DISTRIBUTES RECORDINGS of the internationally acclaimed choir *Gloriæ Dei Cantores*, the *Gloriæ Dei Cantores Schola*, and the other instrumental artists of the *Arts Empowering Life Foundation*.

PARACLETE PRESS IS THE EXCLUSIVE NORTH AMERICAN DISTRIBUTOR for the Gregorian chant recordings from St. Peter's Abbey in Solesmes, France. Paraclete also carries all of the Solesmes chant publications for Mass and the Divine Office, as well as their academic research publications.

In addition, PARACLETE PRESS SHEET MUSIC publishes the work of today's finest composers of sacred choral music, annually reviewing over 1,000 works and releasing between 40 and 60 works for both choir and organ.

VIDEO | Our video/DVDs offer spiritual help, healing, and biblical guidance for a broad range of life issues including grief and loss, marriage, forgiveness, facing death, understanding suicide, bullying, addictions, Alzheimer's, and Christian formation.

Learn more about us at our website:
www.paracletepress.com
or phone us toll-free at 1.800.451.5006

SCAN
TO
READ

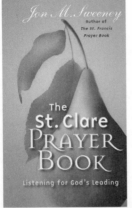